D0180096

5a

A SOLDIER'S PLAY

A Soldier's Play

A PLAY BY

Charles Fuller

A MERMAID DRAMABOOK

HILL AND WANG • NEW YORK
A DIVISION OF FARRAR, STRAUS AND GIROUX

Copyright © 1981 by Charles Fuller
All rights reserved
Published simultaneously in Canada
by McGraw-Hill Ryerson Ltd., Toronto
Printed in the United States of America
First edition, 1982

Library of Congress Cataloging in Publication Data
Fuller, Charles.
A soldier's play.
(A Mermaid dramabook)
I. Title.
PS3556.U367S6 1981   812'.54   82-15395
ISBN 0-8090-8745-6
ISBN 0-8090-1244-8 (pbk.)

CAUTION: Professionals and amateurs are hereby warned that *A Soldier's Play* is subject to a royalty. It is fully protected under the copyright laws of the United States of America, and of all countries covered by the International Copyright Union (including the Dominion of Canada and the rest of the British Commonwealth), and of all countries covered by the Pan-American Copyright Convention and the Universal Copyright Convention, and of all countries with which the United States has reciprocal copyright relations. All rights, including professional, amateur, motion picture, recitation, lecturing, public reading, radio broadcasting, television, and the rights of translation into foreign languages, are strictly reserved. Particular emphasis is laid upon the question of readings, permission for which must be secured from the author's agent in writing.

All inquiries concerning rights (other than stock and amateur rights) should be addressed to William Morris Agency, 1350 Avenue of the Americas, New York, New York 10019.

The stock and amateur production rights for *A Soldier's Play* are controlled exclusively by Samuel French, Inc., 25 West 45th Street, New York, New York 10036. No stock or amateur performance of the play may be given without obtaining in advance the written permission of Samuel French, Inc., and paying the requisite fee.

For LARRY NEAL
whom I will miss
for the rest of my life

A Soldier's Play opened on November 10, 1981, at Theatre Four in New York City. It was presented by the Negro Ensemble Company—Leon B. Denmark, Managing Director, and Douglas Turner Ward, Artistic Director. Direction was by Douglas Turner Ward; scenery by Felix E. Cochren; lighting by Allen Lee Hughes; costumes by Judy Dearing; sound by Regge Life. The cast was as follows:

TECH/SERGEANT VERNON C. WATERS	*Adolph Caesar*
CAPTAIN CHARLES TAYLOR	*Peter Friedman*
CORPORAL BERNARD COBB	*Eugene Lee*
PRIVATE FIRST CLASS MELVIN PETERSON	*Denzel Washington*
CORPORAL ELLIS	*James Pickens, Jr.*
PRIVATE LOUIS HENSON	*Samuel L. Jackson*
PRIVATE JAMES WILKIE	*Steven A. Jones*
PRIVATE TONY SMALLS	*Brent Jennings*
CAPTAIN RICHARD DAVENPORT	*Charles Brown*
PRIVATE C. J. MEMPHIS	*Larry Riley*
LIEUTENANT BYRD	*Cotter Smith*
CAPTAIN WILCOX	*Stephen Zettler*

A SOLDIER'S PLAY

CHARACTERS

TECH/SERGEANT VERNON C. WATERS

CORPORAL BERNARD COBB

PRIVATE JAMES WILKIE

PRIVATE LOUIS HENSON

PFC MELVIN PETERSON

PRIVATE TONY SMALLS

CORPORAL ELLIS

CAPTAIN CHARLES TAYLOR

CAPTAIN RICHARD DAVENPORT

PRIVATE C. J. MEMPHIS

LIEUTENANT BYRD

CAPTAIN WILCOX

ACT ONE

TIME: 1944

PLACE: Fort Neal, Louisiana

SCENE: *The inner shell of the stage is black. On the stage, in a horseshoe-like half circle, are several platforms at varying levels.*

On the left side of this horseshoe is a military office arrangement with a small desk (a nameplate on the desk reads: CAPTAIN CHARLES TAYLOR), *two office-type chairs, one straight-backed, a regimental, and an American flag. A picture of F.D.R. is on the wall.*

On the right side of the horseshoe, and curved toward the rear, is a barracks arrangement, with three bunk beds and footlockers set in typical military fashion. The exit to this barracks is a free-standing doorway on the far right. (This barracks should be changeable—these bunks with little movement can look like a different place.) On the edge of this barracks is a poster, semi-blown up, of Joe Louis in an army uniform, helmet, rifle, and bayonet. It reads: PVT. JOE LOUIS SAYS, "WE'RE GOING TO DO OUR PART—AND WE'LL WIN BECAUSE WE'RE ON GOD'S SIDE."

On the rear of the horseshoe, upstage center, is a bare platform, raised several feet above everything else. It can be anything we want it to be—a limbo if you will.

The entire set should resemble a courtroom. The sets, barracks and office, will both be elevated, so that from anywhere on the horseshoe one may look down onto a space at center stage that is on the stage floor. The levels should have easy access by either stairs or ramps, and the entire set should be raked ever so slightly so that one does not perceive much difference between floor and set, and the bottom edges of the horseshoe. There must also be enough area on both sides of the horseshoe to see exits and entrances.

Lighting will play an integral part in the realization of the play. It should therefore be sharp, so that areas are clearly defined, with as little spill into other areas as possible. Lights must also be capable of suggesting mood, time, and place.

As the play opens, the stage is black. In the background, rising in volume, we hear the song "Don't Sit under the Apple Tree," sung by the Andrews Sisters. Quite suddenly, in a sharp though narrow beam of light, in limbo, TECH/SERGEANT VERNON C. WATERS, a well-built, light-brown-skinned man in a World War II, winter army uniform, is seen down on all fours. He is stinking drunk, trying to stand and mumbling to himself.

WATERS (repeating): They'll still hate you! They still hate you ... They still hate you!

WATERS is laughing as suddenly someone steps into the light. (We never see this person.) He is holding a .45 caliber pistol. He lifts it swiftly and ominously toward WATERS's head and fires. WATERS is knocked over backward. He is dead. The music has stopped and there is a strong silence onstage.

VOICE: Le's go!

The man with the gun takes a step, then stops. He points the gun at WATERS again and fires a second time. There is another silence as limbo is plunged into darkness, and the barracks is just as quickly lit.

We are in the barracks of Company B, 221st Chemical Smoke Generating Company, at Fort Neal. Five black enlisted men *stand at "parade rest" with their hands above their heads and submit to a search. They are:* CORPORAL BERNARD COBB, *a man in his mid to late twenties, dressed in a T-shirt, dog tags, fatigues, and slippers.* PRIVATE JAMES WILKIE, *a man in his early forties, a career soldier, is dressed in fatigues from which the stripes have been removed, with a baseball cap on, and smoking a cigar.* PRIVATE LOUIS HENSON, *thin, in his late twenties or early thirties, is wearing a baseball T-shirt that reads "Fort Neal" on the front and "#4" on the back, with fatigues and boots on.* PFC MELVIN PETERSON, *a man in his late twenties, wearing glasses, looks angelic. His shirt is open but he does not look sloppy; of all the men, his stripe is the most visible, his boots the most highly polished.* PRIVATE TONY SMALLS, *a man in his late thirties, a career man, is as small as his name feels. All five men are being searched by* CORPORAL ELLIS, *a soldier who is simply always "spit and polish."* ELLIS *is also black, and moves from man to man, patting them down in a police-like search.* CAPTAIN CHARLES TAYLOR, *a young white man in his mid to late thirties, looks on, a bit disturbed. All the men's uniforms are from World War II.*

TAYLOR: I'm afraid this kind of thing can't be helped, men—you can put your arms down when Ellis finishes. (*Several men drop their arms.* ELLIS *is searching* PVT. HENSON) We don't want anyone from Fort Neal going into Tynin looking for red-necks.

COBB: May I speak, sir? (TAYLOR *nods*) Why do this, Captain? They got M.P.'s surrounding us, and hell, the Colonel must know nobody colored killed the man!

TAYLOR: This is a precaution, Cobb. We can't have revenge killings, so we search for weapons.

PETERSON: Where'd they find the Sarge, sir?

TAYLOR: In the woods out by the Junction—and so we don't have any rumors. Sergeant Waters was shot twice—we don't know that he was lynched! (*Pause*) Twice. Once in the chest, and a bullet in the head. (ELLIS *finishes with the last man*) You finished the footlockers?

ELLIS: Yes, sir! There aren't any weapons.

TAYLOR (*relaxes*): I didn't think there would be. At ease, men! (*The men relax*) Tech/Sergeant Waters, in my opinion, served the 221st and this platoon in particular with distinction, and I for one shall miss the man. (*Slight pause*) But no matter what we think of the Sergeant's death, we will not allow this incident to make us forget our responsibility to this uniform. We are soldiers, and our war is with the Nazis and Japs, not the civilians in Tynin. Any enlisted man found with unauthorized weapons will be immediately subject to summary court-martial. (*Softens*) Sergeant Waters's replacement won't be assigned for several weeks. Until that time, you will all report to Sergeant Dorsey of C Company. Corporal Cobb will be barracks N.C.O. —any question?

PETERSON: Who do they think did it, sir?

TAYLOR: At this time there are no suspects.

HENSON: You know the Klan did it, sir.

TAYLOR: Were you an eyewitness, soldier?

HENSON: Who else goes around killin' Negroes in the South?— They lynched Jefferson the week I got here, sir! And that Signal Corps guy, Daniels, two months later!

TAYLOR: Henson, unless you saw it, keep your opinions to yourself! Is that clear? (HENSON *nods*) And that's an order! It also applies to everybody else!

ALL (*almost simultaneously*): Yes, sir!

TAYLOR: You men who have details this afternoon, report to the orderly room for your assignments. The rest of you are assigned to the Colonel's quarters—clean-up detail. Cobb, I want to see you in my office at 1350 hours.

COBB: Yes, sir.

TAYLOR: As of 0600 hours this morning, the town of Tynin was placed off-limits to all military personnel. (*Slight groan from the men*) The Friday night dance has also been canceled— (*All the men moan.* TAYLOR *is sympathetic*) O.K., O.K.! Some of the officers are going to the Colonel—I can't promise anything. Right now, it's canceled.

ELLIS: Tenn-hut!

The men snap to. The CAPTAIN *salutes. Only* COBB *salutes him back. The* CAPTAIN *starts out.*

TAYLOR: As you were!

The CAPTAIN *and* ELLIS *exit the barracks. The men move to their bunks or footlockers.* WILKIE *goes to the rear of the bunks and looks out.*

COBB: They still out there, Wilkie?

WILKIE: Yeah. Got the whole place surrounded.

HENSON: I don't know what the hell they thought we'd go into that town with—mops and dishrags?

WILKIE: Y'all recruits know what Colonel's clean-up detail is, don't you? Shovelin' horseshit in his stables—

COBB: Ain't no different from what we been doin'. (*He lies down and begins scratching around his groin area*)

PETERSON (*to* COBB): Made you the barracks Commander-in-Chief, huh? (COBB *nods*) Don't git like ole Stone-ass— What are you doin'?

COBB: Scratchin'!

HENSON (*overlapping*): Taylor knows the Klan did it—I hope y'all know that!

SMALLS (*sudden*): Then why are the M.P.'s outside with rifles? Why hold us prisoner?

PETERSON: They scared we may kill a couple peckerwoods, Smalls. Calm down, man!

WILKIE (*quickly*): Smalls, you wanna play some coon-can?

SMALLS *shakes his head no. He is quiet, staring.*

COBB (*examining himself*): Peterson, you know I think Eva gave me the crabs.

HENSON: Cobb, the kinda women you find, it's a wonda your nuts ain't fell off—crabs? You probably got lice, ticks, bedbugs, fleas—tapeworms—

COBB: Shut up, Henson! Pete—I ain't foolin', man! (*He starts to open his pants*)

PETERSON: Get some powder from the PX.

WILKIE (*almost simultaneously*): Which one of y'all feels like playin' me some cards? (*He looks at* HENSON)

HENSON: Me and Peterson's goin' down the mess hall—you still goin', Pete?

PETERSON (*nods*): Wilkie? I thought all you could do was play go-fer?

HENSON (*slyly*): Yeah, Wilkie—whose ass can you kiss, now that your number-one ass is dead?

COBB (*laughing*): That sounds like something C.J. would sing! (*Looks at himself again*) Ain't this a bitch? (*Picks at himself*)

WILKIE (*overlapping, to* HENSON): You know what you can do for me, Henson—you too, Peterson!

PETERSON: Naughty, naughty!

WILKIE *moves to his bunk, justifying.*

WILKIE: I'm the one lost three stripes—and I'm the only man in here with kids, so when the man said jump, I jumped!

HENSON (*derisively*): Don't put your wife and kids between you and Waters's ass, man!

WILKIE: I wanted my stripes back!

COBB: I'm goin' to sick call after chow.

WILKIE (*continuing*): Y'all ain't neva' had nothin', that's why you can't understand a man like me! There was a time I was a sergeant major, you know!

HENSON *waves disdainfully at him, turning his attention to* COBB

HENSON: Ole V-girl slipped Cobb the crabs! How you gonna explain that to the girl back home, Corporal? How will that fine, big-thighed Moma feel, when the only ribbon you bring home from this war is the Purple Heart for crab bites? (HENSON *laughs as* SMALLS *stands suddenly*)

SMALLS: Don't any of you guys give a damn?

PETERSON: What's the matta', Smalls?

SMALLS: The man's dead! We saw him alive last night!

COBB (*quickly*): I saw him, too. At least I know he died good and drunk!

SMALLS (*loud*): What's the matter with y'all?

HENSON: The man got hisself lynched! We're in the South, and we can't do a goddamn thing about it—you heard the Captain! But don't start actin' like we guilty of somethin'. (*Softens*) I just hope we get lucky enough to get shipped outta this hell-hole to the war! (*To himself*) Besides, whoever did it, didn't kill much anyway.

SMALLS: He deserved better than that!

COBB: Look, everybody feels rotten, Smalls. But it won't bring the man back, so let's forget about it!

PETERSON *moves to pat* SMALLS *on the back.*

PETERSON: Why don't you walk it off, man?

SMALLS *moves away to his bunk.* PETERSON *shrugs.*

HENSON: Yeah—or go turn on a smoke machine, let the fog make you think you in London!

SMALLS *sits down on his bunk and looks at them for a moment, then lays down, his face in the pillow.*

WILKIE (*overlapping*): Let Cobb bring his Eva over, she'll take his mind off Waters plus give him a bonus of crabs!

The men laugh, but SMALLS *doesn't move as the lights begin slowly to fade out.*

HENSON (*counting*): —an' blue-balls. Clap. Syphilis. Pimples! (COBB *throws a pillow at* HENSON) Piles! Fever blisters. Cock-eyes. Cooties!

The men are laughing as the lights go out. As they do, a rather wiry black officer wearing glasses, CAPTAIN RICHARD DAVENPORT,

*walks across the stage from the wings, dressed sharply in an M.P.
uniform, his hat cocked to the side and strapped down, the way
airmen wear theirs. He is carrying a briefcase, and we are aware
of a man who is very confident and self-assured. He is smiling as
he faces the audience, cleaning his glasses as he begins to speak.*

DAVENPORT: Call me Davenport—Captain, United States Army,
    attached to the 343rd Military Police Corps Unit, Fort Neal,
    Louisiana. I'm a lawyer the segregated Armed Services couldn't
    find a place for. My job in this war? Policing colored troops.
    (*Slight pause*) One morning, during mid-April 1944, a colored
    tech/sergeant, Vernon C. Waters, assigned to the 221st Chem-
    ical Smoke Generating Company, stationed here before transfer
    to Europe, was brutally shot to death in a wooded section off
    the New Post Road and the junction of Highway 51—just
    two hundred yards from the colored N.C.O. club—by a person
    or persons unknown. (*Pauses a little*) Naturally, the unofficial
    consensus was the local Ku Klux Klan, and for that reason,
    I was told at the time, Colonel Barton Nivens ordered the
    Military Police to surround the enlisted men's quarters—then
    instructed all his company commanders to initiate a thorough
    search of all personal property for unauthorized knives, guns—
    weapons of any kind. (*Slight pause*) You see, ninety percent
    of the Colonel's command—all of the enlisted men stationed
    here are Negroes, and the Colonel felt—and I suppose justly—
    that once word of the Sergeant's death spread among his troops,
    there might be some retaliation against the white citizens of
    Tynin. (*Shrugs*) What he did worked—there was no retaliation,
    and no racial incidents. (*Pause*) The week after the killing
    took place, several correspondents from the Negro press wrote
    lead articles about it. But the headlines faded—(*Smiles*) The
    NAACP got me involved in this. Rumor has it, Thurgood
    Marshall ordered an immediate investigation of the killing,

and the army, pressured by Secretary of War Stimson, rather randomly ordered Colonel Nivens to initiate a preliminary inquiry into the Sergeant's death. Now, the Colonel didn't want to rehash the murder, but he complied with the army's order by instructing the Provost Marshal, my C.O., Major Hines, to conduct a *few* question-and-answer sessions among the men of Sergeant Waters's platoon and file a report. The matter was to be given the lowest priority. (*Pause*) The case was mine, five minutes later. It was four to five weeks after his death—the month of May. (*He pauses as the light builds in* CAPTAIN TAYLOR's *office.* TAYLOR *is facing* DAVENPORT, *expressionless.* DAVENPORT *is a bit puzzled*) Captain?

TAYLOR: Forgive me for occasionally staring, Davenport, you're the first colored officer I've ever met. I'd heard you had arrived a month ago, and you're a bit startling. (*Quickly*) I mean you no offense. (*Starts back to his desk and sits on the edge of it, as* DAVENPORT *starts into the office a bit cautiously*) We'll be getting some of you as replacements, but we don't expect them until next month. Sit down, Davenport. (DAVENPORT *sits*) You came out of Fort Benning in '43?

DAVENPORT: Yes.

TAYLOR: And they assigned a lawyer to the Military Police? I'm Infantry and I've been with the Engineers, Field Artillery, and Signal Corps—this is some army. Where'd you graduate law school?

DAVENPORT: Howard University.

TAYLOR: Your daddy a rich minister or something? (DAVENPORT *shakes his head no*) I graduated the Point— (*Pause*) We didn't have any Negroes at the Point. I never saw a Negro until I was twelve or thirteen. (*Pause*) You like the army, I suppose, huh?

DAVENPORT: Captain, did you see my orders?

TAYLOR (*bristling slightly*): I saw them right after Colonel Nivens sent them to Major Hines. I sent my orderly to the barracks and told him to have the men waiting for you.

DAVENPORT: Thank you.

TAYLOR: I didn't know at the time that Major Hines was assigning a Negro, Davenport. (DAVENPORT *stiffens*) My preparations were made in the belief that you'd be a white man. I think it only fair to tell you that had I known what Hines intended I would have requested the immediate suspension of the investigation— May I speak freely?

DAVENPORT: You haven't stopped yet, Captain.

TAYLOR: Look—how far could you get even if you succeed? These local people aren't going to charge a white man in this parish on the strength of an investigation conducted by a Negro!— and Nivens and Hines know that! The Colonel doesn't give a damn about finding the men responsible for this thing! And they're making a fool of you—can't you see that?—and—take off those sunglasses!

DAVENPORT: I intend to carry out my orders—and I like these glasses—they're like MacArthur's.

TAYLOR: You go near that sheriff's office in Tynin in your uniform—carrying a briefcase, looking and sounding white, and charging local people—and you'll be found just as dead as Sergeant Waters! People around here don't respect the colored!

DAVENPORT: I know that.

TAYLOR (*annoyed*): You know how many times I've asked Nivens to look into this killing? Every day, since it happened, Davenport. Major Hines didn't tell you that!

DAVENPORT: Do you suspect someone, Captain?

TAYLOR: Don't play cat-and-mouse with me, soldier!

DAVENPORT (*calmly*): Captain, like it or not, I'm all you've got. I've been ordered to look into Sergeant Waters's death, and I intend to do exactly that.

There is a long pause.

TAYLOR: Can I tell you a little story? (DAVENPORT *nods*) Before you were assigned here? Nivens got us together after dinner one night, and all we did was discuss Negroes in the officer ranks. We all commanded Negro troops, but nobody had ever come face to face with colored officers—there were a lot of questions that night—for example, your quarters—had to be equal to ours, but we had none—no mess hall for you! (*Slight pause*) Anyway, Jed Harris was the only officer who defended it—my own feelings were mixed. The only Negroes I've ever known were subordinates— My father hired the first Negro I ever saw—man named Colfax—to help him fix the shed one summer. Nice man—worked hard—did a good job, too. (*Remembering; smiles thoughtfully*) But I never met a Negro with any education until I graduated the Point—hardly an officer of equal rank. So I frankly wasn't sure how I'd feel—until right now—and— (*Struggles*) I don't want to offend you, but I just cannot get used to it—the bars, the uniform—being in charge just doesn't look right on Negroes!

DAVENPORT (*rises*): Captain, are you through?

TAYLOR: You could ask Hines for another assignment—this case is not for you! By the time you overcome the obstacles to your race, this case would be dead!

DAVENPORT (*sharply*): I got it. And I *am* in charge! All your orders instruct you to do is cooperate!

There is a moment of silence.

TAYLOR: I won't be made a fool of, Davenport. (*Straightens*) Ellis! You're right, there's no need to discuss this any further.

ELLIS *appears on the edge of the office.*

ELLIS: Yes, sir!

TAYLOR: Captain Davenport will need assistance with the men— I can't prevent that, Davenport, but I intend to do all I can to have this so-called investigation stopped.

DAVENPORT: Do what you like. If there's nothing else, you'll excuse me, won't you, Captain?

TAYLOR (*sardonically*): Glad I met you, Captain.

DAVENPORT *salutes and* TAYLOR *returns salute. For an instant the two men trade cold stares, then* DAVENPORT *gestures to* ELLIS, *and the two of them start out of the office by way of the stage.* DAVENPORT *follows* ELLIS *out. Behind them,* TAYLOR *stares after them as the lights in his office fade out.* DAVENPORT *removes his glasses.*

ELLIS: We heard it was you, sir—you know how the grapevine is. Sad thing—what happened to the Sarge.

DAVENPORT: What's on the grapevine about the killing?

The two men stop as slowly, almost imperceptibly, on the right the barracks area is lit. In it, a small table and two chairs have been set up. ELLIS *shrugs.*

ELLIS: We figure the Klan. They ain't crazy about us tan yanks in this part of the country.

DAVENPORT: Is there anything on the grapevine about trouble in the town before Sergeant Waters was killed?

ELLIS: None that I know of before—after, there were rumors around the post—couple our guys from the Tank Corps wanted to drive them Shermans into Tynin—then I guess you heard that somebody said two officers did it—I figure that's why the Colonel surrounded our barracks.

DAVENPORT: Was the rumor confirmed—I didn't hear that! Did anything ever come of it?

ELLIS: Not that I know of, sir.

DAVENPORT: Thanks, Ellis—I'd better start seeing the men. (*They start into the barracks from the stage floor*) Did you set this up? (ELLIS *nods*) Good— (*He sets his briefcase on the table*) Are they ready?

ELLIS: The Captain instructed everybody in the Sarge's platoon to be here, sir. He told them you'd be starting this morning.

DAVENPORT *smiles.*

DAVENPORT (*to himself*): Before he found out, huh?

ELLIS (*puzzled*): Sir?

DAVENPORT: Nothing. Call the first man in, Corporal—and stay loose, I might need you.

ELLIS: Yes, sir! Sir, may I say something? (DAVENPORT *nods*) It sure is good to see one of us wearin' them Captain's bars, sir.

DAVENPORT: Thank you.

ELLIS *salutes, does a sharp about-face, and starts out.*

ELLIS (*loud*): Private Wilkie!

WILKIE (*offstage*): Yes, sir! (*Almost immediately,* WILKIE *appears in the doorway. He is dressed in proper uniform of fatigues, boots, and cap.*)

ELLIS: Cap'n wants to see you!

WILKIE: Yes indeedy! (*Moves quickly to the table, where he comes to attention and salutes*) Private James Wilkie reporting as ordered, sir.

DAVENPORT: At ease, Private. Have a seat. (*To* ELLIS *as* WILKIE *sits*) That will be all, Corporal.

ELLIS: Yes, sir.

ELLIS *salutes and exits.* DAVENPORT *waits until he leaves before speaking.*

DAVENPORT: Private Wilkie, I am Captain Davenport—

WILKIE (*interjecting*): Everybody knows that, sir. You all we got down here. (*Smiles broadly*) I was on that first detail got your quarters togetha', sir.

DAVENPORT nods.

DAVENPORT (*coldly*): I'm conducting an investigation into the events surrounding Sergeant Waters's death. Everything you say to me will go in my report, but that report is confidential.

WILKIE: I understand, sir.

DAVENPORT *removes pad and pencil from the briefcase.*

DAVENPORT: How long did you know Sergeant Waters?

WILKIE: 'Bout a year, sir. I met him last March—March 5th—I remember the date, I had been a staff sergeant exactly two years the day after he was assigned. This company was basically a baseball team then, sir. See, most of the boys had played for the Negro League, so naturally the army put us all together. (*Chuckles at the memory*) We'd be assigned to different companies—Motor Pool—Dump Truck all week long—made us do the dirty work on the post—garbage, clean-up—but on Saturdays we were whippin' the hell out of 'em on the baseball diamond! I was hittin' .352 myself! And we had a boy, C. J. Memphis? He coulda hit a ball from Fort Neal to Berlin, Germany—or Tokyo—if he was battin' right-handed. (*Pauses, catches* DAVENPORT's *impatience*) Well, the army sent Waters to manage the team. He had been in Field Artillery—Gunnery Sergeant. Had a croix de guerre from the First War, too.

DAVENPORT: What kind of man was he?

WILKIE: All spit and polish, sir.

At that moment, in limbo, a spotlight hits SERGEANT WATERS. *He is dressed in a well-creased uniform, wearing a helmet liner and standing at parade-rest, facing the audience. The light around him, however, is strange—it is blue-gray like the past. The light around* DAVENPORT *and* WILKIE *abates somewhat. Dialogue is continuous.*

DAVENPORT: Tell me about him.

WILKIE: He took my stripes! (*Smiles*) But I was in the wrong, sir!

WATERS *stands at ease. His voice is crisp and sharp, his movements minimal. He is the typical hard-nosed N.C.O.—strict, soldierly.*

WATERS: Sergeant Wilkie! You are a noncommissioned officer in the army of a country at war—the penalty for being drunk on duty is severe in peacetime, so don't bring me no po'colored-folks-can't-do-nothin'-unless-they-drunk shit as an excuse! You are supposed to be an example to your men—so, I'm gonna send you to jail for ten days *and* take them goddamn stripes. Teach you a lesson— You in the army! (*Derisively*) Colored folks always runnin' off at the mouth 'bout what y'all gonna do if the white man gives you a chance—and you get it, and what do you do with it? You wind up drunk on guard duty—I don't blame the white man—why the hell should he put colored and white together in this war? You can't even be trusted to guard your own quarters—no wonder they treat us like dogs— Get outta' my sight, *Private!*

Light fades at once on WATERS.

DAVENPORT: What about the other men?

WILKIE: Sometimes the Southern guys caught a little hell—Sarge always said he was from up North somewhere. He was a good soldier, sir. I'm from Detroit myself—born and raised there. Joe Louis started in Detroit—did you know that, sir?

DAVENPORT: What about the Southerners?

WILKIE: Sarge wasn't exactly crazy 'bout 'em—'cept for C.J. Now C.J. was from the South, but with him Sarge was different— probably because C.J. was the best ball player we had. He could sing too! (*Slight pause*) Sarge never got too close to nobody—maybe me—but he didn' mess with C.J., you know what I mean? Not like he did with everybody else.

In limbo the spotlight illuminates C. J. MEMPHIS, *a young, hand-some black man. He is in a soldier's uniform, cap on the side. He is strumming a guitar.* WATERS *is watching him, smiling. Their light is the strange light of the past.* C.J. *begins to sing, his voice deep, melodious, and bluesy.*

C.J.: It's a low/it's a low, low/lowdown dirty shame! Yeah, it's a low/it's a low, low/lowdown dirty shame!

WILKIE (*before* C.J. *finishes*): Big Mississippi boy!

WILKIE *and* C.J. *simultaneously sing.*

C.J. AND WILKIE: They say we fightin' Hitler! But they won't let us in the game!

C.J. *strums and hums as* WATERS *looks on.*

WILKIE: Worked harder and faster than everybody—wasn' a man on the team didn't like him. Sarge took to him the first time he saw him. "Wilkie," he says.

WILKIE AND WATERS (*simultaneously*): What have we got here?

WATERS: A guitar-playin' man! Boy, you eva' heard of Blind Willie Reynolds? Son House? Henry Sims?

C.J. *nods to everything.*

C.J.: You heard them play, Sarge?

WATERS: Every one of 'em. I was stationed in Mississippi couple years ago—you from down that way, ain't you?

C.J.: Yes, sah!

WATERS: Well, they use ta play over at the Bandana Club outside Camp J. J. Reilly.

C.J.: I played there once!

WATERS (*smiles*): Ain't that somethin'? I'd go over there from time to time—people use ta come from everywhere! (*To* WILKIE) Place was always dark, Wilkie—smoky. Folks would be dancin'—sweatin'—guitar pickers be strummin', shoutin'— it would be wild in there sometimes. Reminded me of a place I use ta go in France durin' the First War—the women, the whiskey—place called the Café Napoleon.

C.J.: You really like the blues, huh?

WATERS: No other kind of music—where'd you learn to play so good? I came by here yesterday and heard this pickin'—one of the men tol' me it was you.

C.J.: My daddy taught me, Sarge.

WATERS: You play pretty good, boy. Wilkie, wasn' that good?

WILKIE: Yes indeed, Sarge.

WILKIE (*to Davenport*): I mostly agreed with the Sarge, sir. He was a good man. Good to his men. Talked about his wife and kids all the time— (WATERS *starts down from the limbo area, as the lights around* C.J. *fade out.* WATERS *pulls a pipe from his pocket, lights it as he moves to the edge of the* CAPTAIN's *office and sits on the edge of the platform supporting it. He puffs a*

few times. WILKIE's *talk is continuous*) Use ta write home every
day. I don't see why nobody would want to kill the Sarge, sir.

WATERS *smiles.*

WATERS: Wilkie? (WILKIE *rises and walks into the blue-gray light
and the scene with* WATERS. DAVENPORT *will watch*) You know
what I'ma get that boy of mine for his birthday? One of them
Schwinn bikes. He'll be twelve—time flies, don't it? Let me
show you something?

WILKIE (*to* DAVENPORT): He was always pullin' out snapshots, sir.

WATERS *hands him a snapshot.*

WATERS: My wife let a neighbor take this a couple weeks ago—
ain't he growin' fast?

WILKIE: He's over your wife's shoulder! (*Hands it back.* WATERS
looks at the photo)

WATERS: I hope this kid never has to be a soldier.

WILKIE: It was good enough for you.

WATERS: I couldn't do any better—and this army was the closest
I figured the white man would let me get to any kind of authority. No, the army ain't for this boy. When this war's over,
things are going to change, Wilkie—and I want him to be
ready for it—my daughter, too! I'm sendin' bot' of 'em to some
big white college—let 'em rub elbows with the whites, learn
the white man's language—how he does things. Otherwise,

we'll be left behind—you can see it in the army. White man runnin' rings around us.

WILKIE: A lot of us didn't get the chance or the schoolin' the white folks got.

WATERS: That ain't no excuse, Wilkie. Most niggahs just don't care—tomorrow don't mean nothin' to 'em. My daddy shoveled coal from the back of a wagon all his life. He couldn't read or write, but he saw to it we did! Not havin' ain't no excuse for not gettin'.

WILKIE: Can't get pee from a rock, Sarge.

WATERS *rises abruptly*.

WATERS: You just like the rest of 'em, Wilkie—I thought bustin' you would teach you something—we got to challenge this man in his arena—use his weapons, don't you know that? We need lawyers, doctors—generals—senators! Stop thinkin' like a niggah!

WILKIE: All I said—

WATERS: Is the equipment ready for tomorrow's game?

WILKIE: Yeah.

WATERS: Good. You can go now, Wilkie. (WILKIE *is stunned*) That's an order!

WILKIE *turns toward* DAVENPORT. *In the background, the humming of* C.J. *rises a bit as the light around* WATERS *fades out.*

WILKIE: He could be two people sometimes, sir. Warm one minute—ice the next.

DAVENPORT: How did you feel about him?

WILKIE: Overall—I guess he was all right. You could always borrow a ten-spot off him if you needed it.

DAVENPORT: Did you see the Sergeant any time immediately preceding his death?

WILKIE: I don't know how much before it was, but a couple of us had been over the N.C.O. club that night and Sarge had been juicin' pretty heavy.

DAVENPORT: Did Waters drink a lot?

WILKIE: No more than most— (*Pause*) Could I ask you a question, sir? (DAVENPORT *nods*) Is it true, when they found Sarge all his stripes and insignia were still on his uniform?

DAVENPORT: I don't recall it being mentioned in my preliminary report. Why?

WILKIE: If that's the way they found him, something's wrong, ain't it, sir? Them Klan boys don't like to see us in these uniforms. They usually take the stripes and stuff off, before they lynch us.

DAVENPORT *is quiet, thoughtful for a moment.*

DAVENPORT: Thank you, Private—I might want to call you again, but for now you're excused.

WILKIE *rises.*

WILKIE: Yes, sir! (*Sudden mood swing, hesitant*) Sir?

DAVENPORT: Yes?

WILKIE: Can you do anything about allotment checks? My wife didn' get hers last month.

DAVENPORT: There's nothing I can do directly—did you see the finance officer? (WILKIE *nods*) Well—I'll—I'll mention it to Captain Taylor.

WILKIE: Thank you, sir. You want me to send the next man in?

DAVENPORT *nods.* WILKIE *salutes, does an about-face, and exits.* DAVENPORT *returns the salute, then leans back in his chair thoughtfully. In the background, the humming of* C.J. *rises again as the next man,* PFC MELVIN PETERSON, *enters. Dressed in fatigues, he is the model soldier. He walks quickly to the table, stands at attention, and salutes. The humming fades out as* DAVENPORT *returns the salute.*

PETERSON: Private First Class Melvin Peterson reporting as ordered, sir!

DAVENPORT: Sit down, Private. (PETERSON *sits*) Do you know why I'm here?

PETERSON: Yes, sir.

DAVENPORT: Fine. Now, everything you tell me is confidential, so

I want you to speak as freely as possible. (PETERSON *nods*) Where are you from?

PETERSON: Hollywood, California—by way of Alabama, sir. I enlisted in '42—thought we'd get a chance to fight.

DAVENPORT (*ignores the comment*): Did you know Sergeant Waters well?

PETERSON: No, sir. He was already with the company when I got assigned here. And us common G.I.'s don't mix well with N.C.O.'s.

DAVENPORT: Were you on the baseball team?

PETERSON: Yes, sir—I played shortstop.

DAVENPORT: Did you like the Sergeant?

PETERSON: No, sir.

Before DAVENPORT *can speak,* ELLIS *enters.*

ELLIS: Beg your pardon, sir. Captain Taylor would like to see you in his office at once.

DAVENPORT: Did he say why?

ELLIS: No, sir—just that you should report to him immediately.

DAVENPORT (*annoyed*): Tell the men to stick around. When I finish with the Captain, I'll be back.

ELLIS: Yes, sir!

ELLIS *exits.*

DAVENPORT (*to* PETERSON): Feel like walking, Private? We can continue this on the way. (*Begins to put his things in his briefcase*) Why didn't you like the Sergeant?

DAVENPORT *and* PETERSON *start out as the light begins to fade in the barracks. They go through doorway, exit, and reenter the stage in full view.*

PETERSON: It goes back to the team, sir. I got here in—baseball season had started, so it had to be June—June of last year. The team had won maybe nine—ten games in a row, there was a rumor that they would even get a chance to play the Yankees in exhibition. So when I got assigned to a team like that, sir— I mean, I felt good. Anyway, ole Stone-ass—

DAVENPORT: Stone-ass?

PETERSON: I'm the only one called him that—Sergeant Waters, sir.

As the two of them pass in front of the barracks area, the light begins to rise very slowly, but it is the blue-gray light of the past. The chairs and table are gone, and the room looks different.

DAVENPORT: Respect his rank, with me, Private.

PETERSON: I didn't mean no offense, sir. (*Slight pause*) Well, the Sergeant and that brown-nosin' Wilkie? They ran the team— and like it was a chain gang, sir. A chain gang!

The two men exit the stage. As they do, C.J. MEMPHIS, HENSON,
COBB, *and* SMALLS *enter in their baseball uniforms. T-shirts with
"Fort Neal" stamped on the fronts, and numbers on the back,
and baseball caps. They are carrying equipment—bats, gloves.*
C.J. *is carrying his guitar.* SMALLS *enters tossing a baseball into
the air and catching it. They almost all enter at once, with the
exuberance of young men. Their talk is locker-room loud, and
filled with bursts of laughter.*

HENSON: You see the look on that umpire's face when C.J. hit
that home run? I thought he was gonna die on the spot, he
turned so pale!

They move to their respective bunks.

SMALLS: Serves the fat bastard right! Some of them pitches he
called strikes were well ova' my head!

C.J. *strums his guitar.* COBB *begins to brush off his boots.*

COBB: C.J.? Who was that fine, river-hip thing you was talkin' to,
homey?

C.J. *shrugs and smiles.*

HENSON: Speakin' of women, I got to write my Lady a letter. (*He
begins to dig for his writing things*)

COBB: She looked mighty good to me, C.J.

SMALLS (*overlapping*): Y'all hear Henson? Henson, you ain't had
a woman since a woman had you!

HENSON *makes an obscene gesture.*

C.J. (*overlapping* SMALLS): Now, all she did was ask me for my autograph.

COBB: Look like she was askin' you fo' mor'n that. (*To* SMALLS) You see him, Smalls? Leanin' against the fence, all in the woman's face, breathin' heavy—

HENSON: If Smalls couldn't see enough to catch a ground ball right in his glove, how the hell could he see C.J. ova' by the fence?

SMALLS: That ball got caught in the sun!

HENSON: On the ground?

COBB (*at once*): We beat 'em nine to one! Y'all be quiet, I'm askin' this man 'bout a woman he was with had tits like two helmets!

C.J.: If I had'a give that gal what she asked fo'—she'da give me somethin' I didn' want! Them V-gals git you a bad case a' clap. 'Sides, she wasn' but sixteen.

SMALLS: You shoulda introduced her to Henson—sixteen's about his speed.

HENSON *makes a farting sound in retaliation.*

C.J.: Aroun' home? There's a fella folks use ta call, Lil' Jimmy One Leg—on account of his thing was so big? Two years ago—

ole young pretty thing laid clap on Jimmy so bad, he los' the one good leg he had! Now folks jes' call him Little!

Laughter.

c.j.: That young thing talkin' to me ain' look so clean.

HENSON: Dirty or clean, she had them white boys lookin'.

COBB: Eyes popin' out they sockets, wasn' they? Remind me of that pitcher las' week! The one from 35th Ordnance? The one everybody claimed was so good? Afta' twelve straight hits, he looked the same way!

PETERSON *enters, carrying two baseball bats.*

SMALLS: It might be funny ta y'all, but when me and Pete had duty in the Ordnance mess hall, that same white pitcher was the first one started the name-callin'—

HENSON: Forget them dudes in Ordnance—lissen to this! (HENSON *begins to read from a short letter*) "Dear, Louis"—y'all hear that? The name is Louis—

COBB: Read the damn letter!

HENSON (*makes obscene gesture*): "Dear, Louis. You and the boys keep up the good work. All of us here at home are praying for you and inspired in this great cause by you. We know the Nazis and the Japs can't be stopped unless we all work together, so tell your buddies to press forward and win this war. All our hopes for the future go with you, Louis. Love Mattie."

I think I'm in love with the sepia Winston Churchill—what kinda' letter do you write a nut like this?

COBB: Send her a round of ammunition and a bayonet, *Louis!*

HENSON *waves disdainfully.*

PETERSON: Y'all oughta listen to what Smalls said. Every time we beat them at baseball, they get back at us every way they can.

COBB: It's worth it to me just to wipe those superior smiles off they faces.

PETERSON: I don't know—seems like it makes it that much harder for us.

C.J.: They tell me, coupla them big-time Negroes is on the verge a' gittin' all of us togetha'—colored and white—say they want one army.

PETERSON: Forget that, C.J.! White folks'll neva' integrate no army!

C.J. (*strums*): If they do—I'ma be ready for 'em! (*Sings*) Well, I got me a bright red zoot suit / And a pair a' patent-leatha' shoes / And my woman she sittin' waitin' / Fo' the day we hea' the news! Lawd, lawd, lawd, lawd, / Lawd, lawd, lawd, lawd!

SERGEANT WATERS, *followed by* WILKIE, *enters, immediately crossing to the center of the barracks, his strident voice abruptly cutting off* C.J.'s *singing and playing.*

WATERS: Listen up! (*To* C.J.) We don't need that guitar playin'-sittin'-round-the-shack music today, C.J.! (*Smiles*) I want all you men out of those baseball uniforms and into work clothes! You will all report to me at 1300 hours in front of the Officers Club. We've got a work detail. We're painting the lobby of the club.

Collective groan.

SMALLS: The officers can't paint their own club?

COBB: Hell no, Smalls! Let the great-colored-clean-up company do it! Our motto is: Anything you don't want to do, the colored troops will do for you!

HENSON (*like a cheer*): Anything you don't want to do, the colored troops will do for you! (*He starts to lead the others*)

OTHERS: Anything you don't—

WATERS: That's enough!

The men are instantly silent.

HENSON: When do we get a rest? We just played nine innings of baseball, Sarge!

SMALLS: We can't go in the place, why the hell should we paint it?

COBB: Amen, brother!

There is a moment of quiet before WATERS *speaks.*

WATERS: Let me tell you fancy-assed ball-playin' Negroes somethin'! The *reasons* for any orders given by a superior officer is none of y'all's business! You obey them! This country is at war, and you niggahs are soldiers—nothin' else! So baseball teams—win or lose—get no special privileges! They need to work some of you niggahs till your legs fall off! (*Intense*) And something else—from now on, when I tell you to do something, I want it done—is that clear? (*The men are quiet*) Now, Wilkie's gonna' take all them funky shirts you got on over to the laundry. I could smell you suckers before I hit the field!

PETERSON: What kinda colored man are you?

WATERS: I'm a soldier, Peterson! First, last, and always! I'm the kinda colored man that don't like lazy, shiftless Negroes!

PETERSON: You ain't got to come in here and call us names!

WATERS: The Nazis call you schvatza! You gonna tell them they hurt your little feelings?

C.J.: Don't look like to me we could do too much to them Nazis wit' paint brushes, Sarge.

The men laugh. The moment is gone, and though WATERS *is angry, his tone becomes overly solicitous, smiling.*

WATERS: You tryin' to mock me, C.J.?

C.J.: No, sah, Sarge.

WATERS: Good, because whatever an ignorant, low-class geechy like you has to say isn't worth paying attention to, is it? (*Pause*) Is it?

c.j.: I reckon not, Sarge.

PETERSON: You' a creep, Waters!

WATERS: Boy, you are something—ain't been in the company a month, Wilkie, and already everybody's champion!

c.j. (*interjecting*): Sarge was just jokin', Pete—he don't mean no harm!

PETERSON: He does! We take enough from the white boys!

WATERS: Yes, you do—and if it wasn' for you Southern niggahs, yessahin', bowin' and scrapin', scratchin' your heads, white folks wouldn' think we were all fools!

PETERSON: Where you from, England?

Men snicker.

HENSON (*at once*): Peterson!

WATERS (*immediately*): You got somethin' to say, Henson?

HENSON: Nothin', Sarge.

HENSON *shakes his head as* WATERS *turns back to* PETERSON.

WATERS: Peterson, you got a real comic streak in you. Wilkie, looks like we got us a wise-ass Alabama boy here! (*He moves toward* PETERSON) Yes, sir— (*He snatches* PETERSON *in the collar*) Don't get smart, niggah!

PETERSON *yanks away.*

PETERSON: Get your fuckin' hands off me!

WATERS *smiles, leans forward.*

WATERS: You wanna hit ole Sergeant Waters, boy? (*Whispers*) Come on! Please! Come on, niggah!

CAPTAIN TAYLOR *enters the barracks quite suddenly, unaware of what is going on.*

HENSON: Tenn-hut!

All the men snap to.

TAYLOR: At ease! (*He moves toward* WATERS, *feeling the tension*) What's going on here, Sergeant?

WATERS: Nothin', sir—I was going over the *Manual of Arms.* Is there something in particular you wanted, sir? Something I can do?

TAYLOR (*relaxed somewhat*): Nothing— (*To the men*) Men, I congratulate you on the game you won today. We've only got seven more to play, and if we win them, we'll be the first team in Fort Neal history to play the Yanks in exhibition. Everyone in the regiment is counting on you. In times like these, morale is important—and winning can help a lot of things. (*Pause*)

Sergeant, as far as I'm concerned, they've got the rest of the day off.

The men are pleased.

WATERS: Begging your pardon, sir, but these men need all the work they can get. They don't need time off—our fellas aren't getting time off in North Africa—besides, we've got orders to report to the Officers Club for a paint detail at 1300 hours.

TAYLOR: Who issued that order?

WATERS: Major Harris, sir.

TAYLOR: I'll speak to the Major.

WATERS: Sir, I don't think it's such a good idea to get a colored N.C.O. mixed up in the middle of you officers, sir.

TAYLOR: I said, I'd speak to him, Sergeant.

WATERS: Yes, sir!

TAYLOR: I respect the men's duty to service, but they need time off.

WATERS: Yes, sir.

Pause.

TAYLOR: You men played a great game of baseball out there today —that catch you made in center field, Memphis—how the hell'd you get up so high?

c.j. (*shrugs, smiles*): They say I got "Bird" in mah blood, sir.

TAYLOR *is startled by the statement, his smile is an uncomfortable one.* WATERS *is standing on "eggs."*

TAYLOR: American eagle, I hope. (*Laughs a little*)

c.j.: No, sah, crow— (WATERS *starts to move, but* c.j. *stops him by continuing. Several of the men are beginning to get uncomfortable*) Man tol' my daddy the day I was born, the shadow of a crow's wings—

TAYLOR (*cutting him off*): Fine—men, I'll say it again—you played superbly. (*Turns to* WATERS) Sergeant. (*He starts out abruptly*)

WATERS: Tenn-hut!

WATERS *salutes as the men snap to.*

TAYLOR (*exiting*): As you were.

TAYLOR *salutes as he goes. There is an instant of quiet. The men relax a little, but their focus is* c.j.

WATERS (*laughing*): Ain't these geechies somethin'? How long a story was you gonna tell the man, C.J.? My God! (*The men join him, but as he turns toward* PETERSON, *he stiffens*) Peterson! Oh, I didn't forget you, boy. (*The room quiets*) It's time to teach you a lesson!

PETERSON: Why don't you drop dead, Sarge?

WATERS: Nooo! I'ma drop you, boy! Out behind the barracks—
Wilkie, you go out and make sure it's all set up.

WILKIE: You want all the N.C.O.'s?

WATERS *nods.* WILKIE *goes out smiling.*

WATERS: I'm going outside and wait for you, geechy! And when
you come out, I'm gonna whip your black Southern ass—let
the whole company watch it, too! (*Points*) You need to learn
respect, boy—how to talk to your betters. (*Starts toward the
door*) Fight hard, hea'? I'ma try to bust your fuckin' head open
—the rest of you get those goddamn shirts off like I said!

He exits. The barracks is quiet for a moment.

COBB: You gonna fight him?

HENSON (*overlapping*): I tried to warn you!

PETERSON: You ain't do nothin'!

SMALLS: He'll fight you dirty, Pete—don't do it!

PETERSON *goes to his bunk and throws his cap off angrily.*

COBB: You don't want to do it?

PETERSON: You wanna fight in my place, Cobb? (*He sits*) Shit!

Slight pause. HENSON *pulls off his shirt.*

C.J.: I got some Farmers Dust—jes' a pinch'll make you strong as a bull—they say it comes from the city of Zar. (*Removes a pouch from his neck*) I seen a man use this stuff and pull a mule outta a sinkhole by hisself!

PETERSON: Get the hell outta here with that backwater crap— can't you speak up for yourself—let that bastard treat you like a dog!

C.J.: 'Long as his han's ain't on me—he ain't done me no harm, Pete. Callin' names ain't nothin', I know what I is. (*Softens*) Sarge ain't so bad—been good to me.

PETERSON: The man despises you!

C.J.: Sarge? You wrong, Pete—plus I feel kinda sorry for him myself. Any man ain't sure where he belongs must be in a whole lotta pain.

PETERSON: Don't y'all care?

HENSON: Don't nobody like it, Pete—but when you here a little longer—I mean, what can you do? This hea's the army and Sarge got all the stripes.

PETERSON *rises, disgusted, and starts out.* SMALLS *moves at once.*

SMALLS: Peterson, look, if you want me to, I'll get the Captain. You don't have to go out there and get your head beat in!

PETERSON: Somebody's got to fight him.

He exits. There is quiet as SMALLS *walks back to his bunk.*

C.J. (*singing*): It's a low / it's a low, low / lowdown dirty shame! It's a low / it's a low, low / lowdown dirty shame! Been playin' in this hea' army / an ain't even learned the game! Lawd, lawd, lawd, lawd—

C.J. *begins to hum as the lights slowly fade out over the barracks. As they do, the lights come up simultaneously in the* CAPTAIN's *office. It is empty.* PETERSON *(in proper uniform) and* DAVENPORT *enter from off-stage. They stop outside the* CAPTAIN's *office.*

PETERSON: He beat me pretty bad that day, sir. The man was crazy!

DAVENPORT: Was the incident ever reported?

PETERSON: I never reported it, sir—I know I should have, but he left me alone after that. (*Shrugs*) I just played ball.

DAVENPORT: Did you see Waters the night he died?

PETERSON: No, sir—me and Smalls had guard duty.

DAVENPORT: Thank you, Private. That'll be all for now. (PETERSON *comes to attention*) By the way, did the team ever get to play the Yankees?

PETERSON: No, sir. We lost the last game to a Sanitation Company.

He salutes. DAVENPORT *returns salute.* PETERSON *does a crisp about-face and exits. Slowly* DAVENPORT *starts into the* CAPTAIN's *office, surprised that no one is about.*

DAVENPORT: Captain? (*There is no response. For a moment or two,* DAVENPORT *looks around. He is somewhat annoyed*) Captain?

He starts out. TAYLOR *enters. He crosses the room to his desk, where he sits.*

TAYLOR: I asked you back here because I wanted you to see the request I've sent to Colonel Nivens to have your investigation terminated. (*He picks up several sheets of paper on his desk and hands them to* DAVENPORT, *who ignores them*)

DAVENPORT: What?

TAYLOR: I wanted you to see that my reasons have nothing to do with you personally—my request will not hurt your army record in any way! (*Pause*) There are other things to consider in this case!

DAVENPORT: Only the color of my skin, Captain.

TAYLOR (*sharply*): I want the people responsible for killing one of my men found and jailed, Davenport!

DAVENPORT: So do I!

TAYLOR: Then give this up! (*Rises*) Whites down here won't see their duty—or justice. They'll see *you!* And once they do, the law—due process—it all goes! And what is the point of continuing an investigation that can't possibly get at the truth?

DAVENPORT: Captain, my orders are very specific, so unless you want charges brought against you for interfering in a criminal investigation, stay the hell out of my way and leave me and my investigation alone!

TAYLOR (*almost sneering*): Don't take yourself too seriously, Davenport. You couldn't find an officer within five hundred miles who would convey charges to a court-martial board against me for something like that, and you know it!

DAVENPORT: Maybe not, but I'd—I'd see to it that your name, rank, and duty station got into the Negro press! Yeah, let a few colored newspapers call you a Negro-hater! Make you an embarrassment to the United States Army, Captain—like Major Albright at Fort Jefferson, and you'd never command troops again—or wear more than those captain's bars on that uniform, Mr. West Point!

TAYLOR: I'll never be more than a captain, Davenport, because I won't let them get away with dismissing things like Waters's death. I've been the commanding officer of three outfits! I raised hell in all of them, so threatening me won't change my request. Let the Negro press print that I don't like being made a fool of with phony investigations!

DAVENPORT (*studies* TAYLOR *for a moment*): There are two white officers involved in this, Captain—aren't there?

TAYLOR: I want them in jail—out of the army! And there is no way *you* can get them charged, or court-martialed, or put away! The white officers on this post won't let you—they won't let me!

DAVENPORT: Why wasn't there any mention of them in your preliminary report? I checked my own summary on the way over here, Captain—nothing! You think I'ma let you get away with this? (*There is a long silence.* TAYLOR *walks back to his desk as* DAVENPORT *watches him.* TAYLOR *sits*) Why?

TAYLOR: I couldn't prove the men in question had anything to do with it.

DAVENPORT: Why didn't you report it?

TAYLOR: I was ordered not to. (*Pause*) Nivens and Hines. The doctors took two .45 caliber bullets out of Waters—army issue. But remember what it was like that morning? If these men had thought a white officer killed Waters, there would have been a slaughter! (*Pause*) Cobb reported the incident innocently the night before—then suddenly it was all over the Fort.

DAVENPORT: Who were they, Captain? I want their names!

TAYLOR: Byrd and Wilcox. Byrd's in Ordnance—Wilcox's with the 12th Hospital Group. I was Captain of the Guard the night Waters was killed. About 2100 hours, Cobb came into my office and told me he'd just seen Waters and two white officers fighting outside the colored N.C.O. club. I called *your* office, and when I couldn't get two M.P.'s, I started over myself to break it up. When I got there—no Waters, no officers. I checked the officers' billet and found Byrd and Wilcox in bed. Several officers verified they'd come in around 2130. I then told Cobb to go back to the barracks and forget it.

DAVENPORT: What made you do that?

TAYLOR: At the time there was no reason to believe anything was

wrong! Waters wasn't found until the following morning. I
told the Colonel what had happened the previous night, and
about the doctor's report, and I was told, since the situation
at the Fort was potentially dangerous, to keep my mouth shut
until it blew over. He agreed to let me question Byrd and Wilcox, but I've asked him for a follow-up investigation every day
since it happened. (*Slight pause*) When I saw you, I exploded
—it was like he was laughing at me.

DAVENPORT: Then you never believed the Klan was involved?

TAYLOR: No. Now, can you see why this thing needs—someone
else?

DAVENPORT: What did they tell you, Captain? Byrd and Wilcox?

TAYLOR: They're not going to let you charge those two men!

DAVENPORT (*snaps*): Tell me what they told you!

TAYLOR *is quiet for a moment. At this time, on center stage in
limbo,* SERGEANT WATERS *is staggering. He is dressed as we first
saw him. Behind him a blinking light reads:* 221st N.C.O. Club.
*As he staggers toward the stairs leading to center stage, two white
officers,* LIEUTENANT BYRD, *a spit-and-polish soldier in his twenties,
and* CAPTAIN WILCOX, *a medical officer, walk on-stage. Both are
in full combat gear—rifles, pistol belts, packs—and both are
tired.* TAYLOR *looks out as if he can see them.*

TAYLOR: They were coming off bivouac.

The two men see WATERS. *In the background is the faint hum of
C.J.'s music.

TAYLOR: They saw him outside the club.

He rises, as WATERS *sees* BYRD *and* WILCOX, *and smiles.*

WATERS: Well, if it ain't the white boys!

WATERS *straightens and begins to march in a mock circle and then down in their direction. He is mumbling, barely audibly:* "One, two, three, four! Hup, hup, three, four! Hup, hup, three, four!" BYRD's *speech overlaps* WATERS's.

BYRD: And it wasn't like we were looking for trouble, Captain— were we, Wilcox?

WILCOX *shakes his head no, but he is astonished by* WATERS's *behavior and stares at him, disbelieving.*

WATERS: White boys! All starched and stiff! Wanted everybody to learn all that symphony shit! That's what you were saying in France—and you know, I listened to you? Am I all right now? Am I?

BYRD: Boy, you'd better straighten up and salute when you see an officer, or you'll find yourself without those stripes! (*To* WILCOX *as* WATERS *nears them, smiling the "coon" smile and doing a juba*) Will you look at this niggah? (*Loud*) Come to attention, Sergeant! That's an order!

WATERS: No, sah! I ain't straightenin' up for y'all no more! I ain't doin' nothin' white folks say do, no more! (*Sudden change of mood, smiles, sings*) No more, no more / no more, no more, noooo! No more, no more / no more, no more, noooooo!

BYRD *faces* TAYLOR *as* WATERS *continues to sing.*

BYRD (*overlapping*): Sir, I thought the man was crazy!

TAYLOR: And what did you think, Wilcox?

BYRD *moves toward* WATERS, *and* WATERS, *still singing low, drunk and staggering, moves back and begins to circle* BYRD, *stalk him, shaking his head no as he sings.* WILCOX *watches apprehensively.*

WILCOX (*at once*): He did appear to be intoxicated, sir—out of his mind almost! (*He turns to* BYRD) Byrd, listen—

BYRD *ignores him.*

DAVENPORT (*suddenly*): Did they see anyone else in the area?

TAYLOR: No. (*To* BYRD) I asked them what they did next.

BYRD: I told that niggah to shut up!

WATERS (*sharply*): No! (*Change of mood*) Followin' behind y'all? Look what it's done to me!—I hate myself!

BYRD: Don't blame us, boy! God made you black, not me!

WATERS (*smiles*): My daddy use ta say—

WILCOX: Sergeant, get hold of yourself!

WATERS (*points*): Listen!

BYRD *steps toward him and shoves him in the face.*

BYRD: I gave you an order, niggah!

WILCOX *grabs* BYRD, *and stops him from advancing, as* WATERS *begins to cry.*

WATERS: My daddy said, "Don't talk like dis'—talk like that!" "Don't live hea'—live there!" (*To them*) I've killed for you! (*To himself; incredulous*) And nothin' changed!

BYRD *pulls free of* WILCOX *and charges* WATERS.

BYRD: He needs to be taught a lesson!

He shoves WATERS *onto the ground, where he begins to beat and kick the man, until he is forcibly restrained by* WILCOX. WATERS *moans.*

WILCOX: Let him be! You'll kill the man! He's sick—leave him alone!

BYRD *pulls away; he is flush.* WATERS *tries to get up.*

WATERS: Nothin' changed—see? And I've tried everything! Everything!

BYRD: I'm gonna bust his black ass to buck private!—I should blow his coward's head off! (*Shouts*) There are good men killing for you, niggah! Gettin' their guts all blown to hell for you!

WILCOX *pulls him away. He pulls* BYRD *off-stage as the light around* WATERS *and that section of the stage begins to fade out. As it does, a trace of* C.J.'s *music is left on the air.* WATERS *is on his knees, groveling, as the lights go out around him.*

DAVENPORT: Did they shove Waters again?

TAYLOR: No. But Byrd's got a history of scrapes with Negroes. They told me they left Waters at 2110—and everyone in the officers' billet verifies they were both in by 2130. And neither man left—Byrd had duty the next morning, and Wilcox was scheduled at the hospital at 0500 hours—both men reported for duty.

DAVENPORT: I don't believe it.

TAYLOR: I couldn't shake their stories—

DAVENPORT: That's nothing more than officers lying to protect two of their own and you know it! I'm going to arrest and charge both of them, Captain—and you may consider yourself confined to your quarters pending my charges against *you!*

TAYLOR: What charges?

DAVENPORT: It was *your* duty to go over Nivens's head if you had to!

TAYLOR: Will you arrest Colonel Nivens too, Davenport? Because he's part of their alibi—he was there when they came in— played poker—from 2100 to 0300 hours the following morning, the Colonel—your Major Hines, "Shack" Callahan—Major Callahan, and Jed Harris—and Jed wouldn't lie for either of them!

DAVENPORT: They're all lying!

TAYLOR: Prove it, hotshot—I told you all I know, now you go out and prove it!

DAVENPORT: I will, Captain! You can bet your sweet ass on that! I will!

DAVENPORT *starts out as the lights begin to fade, and* TAYLOR *looks after him and shakes his head. In the background, the sound of "Don't Sit under the Apple Tree" comes up again and continues to play as the lights fade to black.*

ACT TWO

SCENE: *As before.*

Light rises slowly over limbo. We hear a snippet of "Don't Sit under the Apple Tree" as DAVENPORT, *seated on the edge of a bunk, finishes dressing. He is putting on a shirt, tie, bars, etc., and addresses the audience as he does so.*

DAVENPORT: During May of '44, the Allies were making final preparations for the invasion of Europe. Invasion! Even the sound of it made Negroes think we'd be in it—be swept into Europe in the waves of men and equipment—I know I felt it. (*Thoughtfully*) We hadn't seen a lot of action except in North Africa—or Sicily. But the rumor in orderly rooms that spring was, pretty soon most of us would be in combat—somebody said Ike wanted to find out if the colored boys could fight— shiiit, we'd been fighting all along—right here, in these small Southern towns— (*Intense*) I don't have the authority to arrest a white *private* without a white officer present! (*Slight pause*) Then I get a case like this? There was no way I wouldn't see this through to its end. (*Smiles*) And after my first twenty-four hours, I wasn't doing too badly. I had two prime suspects—a motive, and opportunity! (*Pause*) I went to Colonel Nivens and convinced him that word of Byrd's and Wilcox's involvement couldn't be kept secret any longer. However, before anyone in the press could accuse him of complicity—I would silence all suspicions by pursuing the investigation openly—on his orders— (*Mimics himself*) "Yes, sir, Colonel, you can even send along a white officer—not Captain Taylor, though—I think he's a little too close to the case, sir." Colonel Nivens gave me permission to question Byrd and Wilcox, and having succeeded sooo easily, I decided to spend some time finding out more about Waters and Memphis. Somehow the real drama seemed to be there, and my curiosity wouldn't allow me to ignore it.

DAVENPORT *is dressed and ready to go as a spotlight in the barracks area opens on* PRIVATE HENSON. *He is seated on a footlocker. He rises as* DAVENPORT *descends to the stage. He will not enter the barracks, but will almost handle this like a courtroom interrogation. He returns* HENSON's *salute.*

DAVENPORT: Sit down, Private. Your name is Louis Henson, is that right?

HENSON: Yes, sir.

HENSON *sits, as* DAVENPORT *paces.*

DAVENPORT: Tell me what you know about Sergeant Waters and C. J. Memphis. (HENSON *looks at him strangely*) Is there something wrong?

HENSON: No, sir—I was just surprised you knew about it.

DAVENPORT: Why?

HENSON: You're an officer.

DAVENPORT (*quickly*): And?

HENSON (*hesitantly*): Well—officers are up here, sir—and us enlisted men—down here. (*Slight pause*) C.J. and Waters—that was just between enlisted men, sir. But I guess ain't nothin' a secret around colored folks—not that it was a secret. (*Shrugs*) There ain't that much to tell—sir. Sarge ain't like C.J. When I got to the company in May of las' year, the first person I saw Sarge chew out was C.J.! (*He is quiet*)

DAVENPORT: Go on.

HENSON'*s expression is pained.*

HENSON: Is that an order, sir?

DAVENPORT: Does it have to be?

HENSON: I don't like tattle-talin', sir—an' I don't mean no offense, but I ain't crazy 'bout talkin' to officers—colored or white.

DAVENPORT: It's an order, Henson!

HENSON *nods.*

HENSON: C.J. wasn' movin' fast enough for *him.* Said C.J. didn' have enough *fire-under-his-behind* out on the field.

DAVENPORT: You were on the team?

HENSON: Pitcher. (*Pause.* DAVENPORT *urges with a look*) He jus' *stayed* on C.J. all the time—every little thing, it seemed like to me—then the shootin' went down, and C.J. caught all the hell.

DAVENPORT: What shooting?

HENSON: The shootin' at Williams's Golden Palace, sir—here, las' year!—way before you got here. Toward the end of baseball season. (DAVENPORT *nods his recognition*) The night it happened, a whole lotta gunshots went off near the barracks. I had gotten drunk over at the enlisted men's club, so when I got to the barracks I just sat down in a stupor!

Suddenly shots are heard in the distance and grow ever closer as the eerie blue-gray light rises in the barracks over the sleeping figures of men in their bunks. HENSON *is seated, staring at the ground. He looks up once as the gunshots go off, and as he does, someone—we cannot be sure who—sneaks into the barracks as the men begin to shift and awaken. This person puts something under* C.J.'*s bed and rushes out.* HENSON *watches—surprised at first, rising, then disbelieving. He shakes his head, then sits back down as several men wake up.* DAVENPORT *recedes to one side of the barracks, watching.*

COBB: What the hell's goin' on? Don't they know a man needs his sleep? (*He is quickly back to sleep*)

SMALLS (*simultaneously*): Huh? Who is it? (*Looks around, then falls back to sleep*)

DAVENPORT: Are you sure you saw someone?

HENSON: Well—I saw something, sir.

DAVENPORT: What did you do?

The shooting suddenly stops and the men settle down.

HENSON: I sat, sir—I was juiced— (*Shrugs*) The gunshots weren't any of my business—plus I wasn't sure what I had seen in the first place, then out of nowhere Sergeant Waters, he came in.

WATERS *enters the barracks suddenly, followed by* WILKIE. HENSON *stands immediately, staggering a bit.*

WATERS: All right, all right! Everybody up! Wake them, Wilkie!

WILKIE *moves around the bunks, shaking the men.*

WILKIE: Let's go! Up! Let's go, you guys!

COBB *shoves* WILKIE's *hand aside angrily as the others awaken slowly.*

WATERS: Un-ass them bunks! Tenn-hut! (*Most of the men snap to.* SMALLS *is the last one, and* WATERS *moves menacingly toward him*) There's been a shooting! One of ours bucked the line at Williams's pay phone and three soldiers are dead! Two colored and one white M.P. (*Pauses*) Now, the man who bucked the line, he killed the M.P., and the white boys started shootin' everybody—that's how our two got shot. And this lowdown niggah we lookin' for got chased down here—and was almost caught, 'til somebody in these barracks started shootin' at the men chasin' him. So, we got us a vicious, murderin' piece of black trash in here somewhere—and a few people who helped him. If any of you are in this, I want you to step forward. (*No one moves*) All you baseball niggahs are innocent, huh? Wilkie, make the search. (PETERSON *turns around as* WILKIE *begins*) Eyes front!

PETERSON: I don't want that creep in my stuff!

WATERS: You don't talk at attention!

WILKIE *will search three bunks, top and bottom, along with foot-lockers. Under* C.J.*'s bed he will find what he is looking for.*

WATERS: I almost hope it is some of you geechies—get rid of you Southern niggahs! (*To* WILKIE) Anything yet?

WILKIE: Nawwww!

WATERS: Memphis, are you in this?

C.J.: No, sah, Sarge.

WATERS: How many of you were out tonight?

SMALLS: I was over at Williams's around seven—got me some Lucky Strikes—I didn't try to call home, though.

COBB: I was there, this mornin'!

WATERS: Didn't I say *tonight*—uncle?

WILKIE: Got somethin'!

WILKIE *is holding up a .45 caliber automatic pistol, army issue. Everyone's attention focuses on it. The men are surprised, puzzled.*

WATERS: Where'd you find it?

WILKIE *points to* C.J., *who recoils at the idea.*

c.j.: Naaaawww, man!

waters: C.J.? This yours?

c.j.: You know it ain't mine, Sarge!

waters: It's still warm—how come it's under your bunk?

c.j.: Anybody coulda' put it thea', Sarge!

waters: Who? Or maybe this .45 crawled in through an open window—looked around the whole room—passed Cobb's bunk, and decided to snuggle up under yours? Must be voodoo, right, boy? Or some of that Farmers Dust round that neck of yours, huh?

c.j.: That pistol ain't mine!

waters: Liar!

c.j.: No, Sarge—I hate guns! Make me feel bad jes' to see a gun!

waters: You're under arrest—Wilkie, escort this man to the stockade!

PETERSON *steps forward.*

peterson: C.J. couldn't hurt a fly, Waters, you know that!

waters: I found a gun, soldier—now get out of the way!

peterson: Goddammit, Waters, you know it ain't him!

WATERS: How do I know?

HENSON: Right before you came in, I thought I saw somebody sneak in.

WATERS: You were drunk when you left the club—I saw you myself!

WILKIE: Besides, how you know it wasn't C.J.?

COBB: I was here all night. C.J. didn't go out.

WATERS *looks at them, intense.*

WATERS: We got the right man. (*Points at* C.J., *impassioned*) You think he's innocent, don't you? C. J. Memphis, playin' cottonpicker singin' the blues, bowin' and scrapin'—smilin' in everybody's face—this man undermined us! You and me! The description of the man who did the shooting fits C.J.! (*To* HENSON) You saw C.J. sneak in here! (*Points*) Don't be fooled —that yassah boss is hidin' something—niggahs ain't like that today! This is 1943—he shot that white boy!

C.J. *is stunned, then suddenly the enormity of his predicament hits him and he breaks free of* WILKIE *and hits* WATERS *in the chest. The blow knocks* WATERS *down, and* C.J. *is immediately grabbed by the other men in the barracks.* COBB *goes to* WATERS *and helps him up slowly. The blow hurt* WATERS, *but he forces a smile at* C.J., *who has suddenly gone immobile, surprised by what he has done.*

WATERS: What did you go and do now, boy? Hit a noncommissioned officer.

COBB: Sarge, he didn't mean it!

WATERS: Shut up! (*Straightens*) Take him out, Wilkie.

WILKIE *grabs* C.J. *by the arm and leads him out.* C.J. *goes calmly, almost passively.* WATERS *looks at all the men quietly for a moment, then walks out without saying a word. There is a momentary silence in the barracks.*

SMALLS: Niggah like that can't have a mother.

HENSON: I know I saw something!

PETERSON: C.J. was sleepin' when I came in! It's Waters—can't y'all see that? I've seen him before—we had 'em in Alabama! White man gives them a little ass job as a servant—close to the big house, and when the boss ain't lookin', old copycat niggahs act like they the new owner! They take to soundin' like the boss—shoutin', orderin' people aroun'—and when it comes to you and me—they sell us to continue favor. They think the high-jailers like that. Arrestin' C.J.—that'll get Waters another stripe! Next it'll be you—or you. He can't look good unless he's standin' on you! Cobb tol' him C.J. was in all evening—Waters didn't even listen! Turning somebody in (*mimics*): "Look what I done, Captain Boss!" They let him in the army 'cause they know he'll do anything they tell him to —I've seen his kind of fool before. Someone's going to kill him.

SMALLS: I heard they killed a sergeant at Fort Robinson—recruit did it—

COBB: It'll just be our luck, Sarge'll come through the whole war without a scratch.

PETERSON: Maybe—but I'm goin' over to the stockade—tell the M.P.'s what I know—C.J. was here all evening. (*He starts dressing*)

SMALLS: I'll go with you!

COBB: Me too, I guess.

They all begin to dress as the light fades slowly in the barracks area. HENSON *rises and starts toward* DAVENPORT. *In the background,* C.J.'s *music comes up a bit.*

DAVENPORT: Could the person you thought you saw have stayed in the barracks—did you actually see someone go out?

HENSON: Yes, sir!

DAVENPORT: Was Wilkie the only man out of his bunk that night?

HENSON: Guess so—he came in with Sarge.

DAVENPORT: And Peterson—he did most of the talking?

HENSON: As I recall. It's been a while ago—an' I was juiced!

DAVENPORT *rises.*

DAVENPORT: Ellis!

ELLIS *appears at the door.*

ELLIS: Sir!

DAVENPORT: I want Private Wilkie and Pfc Peterson to report to me at once.

ELLIS: They're probably on work detail, sir.

DAVENPORT: Find them.

ELLIS: Yes, sir!

ELLIS *exits quickly and* DAVENPORT *lapses into a quiet thoughtfulness.*

HENSON: Is there anything else?—Sir?

DAVENPORT (*vexed*): No! That'll be all—send in the next man.

HENSON *comes to attention and salutes.* DAVENPORT *returns salute as* HENSON *exits through the barracks.* C.J.'s *music plays in background. There is a silence.* DAVENPORT *rises, mumbling something to himself.* COBB *appears suddenly at the doorway. He watches* DAVENPORT *for a moment.*

COBB: Sir? (DAVENPORT *faces him*) Corporal Cobb reporting as ordered, sir. (*He salutes*)

DAVENPORT: Have a seat, Corporal (COBB *croses the room and sits*) And let's get something straight from the beginning—I don't care whether you like officers or not—is that clear?

COBB *looks at him strangely.*

COBB: Sir?

Pause. DAVENPORT *calms down somewhat.*

DAVENPORT: I'm sorry— Did you know Sergeant Waters well?

COBB: As well as the next man, sir—I was already with the team when he took over. Me and C.J., we made the team the same time.

DAVENPORT: Were you close to C.J.?

COBB: Me and him were "homeys," sir! Both came from Mississippi. C.J. from Carmella—me, I'm from up 'roun' Jutlerville, what they call snake county. Plus, we both played for the Negro League before the war.

DAVENPORT: How did you feel about his arrest?

COBB: Terrible—C.J. didn't kill nobody, sir.

DAVENPORT: He struck Sergeant Waters—

COBB: Waters made him, sir! He called that boy things he had never heard of before—C.J., he was so confused he didn't know what else to do— (*Pause*) An' when they put him in the stockade, he jus' seemed to go to pieces. (*Lowly in the background,* C.J.'s *music comes up*) See, we both lived on farms—and even though C.J.'s daddy played music, C.J., he liked the wide-open spaces. (*Shakes his head*) That cell? It started closin' in on him right away. (*Blue-gray light rises in limbo, where* C.J. *is sitting on the edge of a bunk. A shadow of bars cuts across the space. His guitar is on the bunk beside him*) I went to see him, the second day he was in there. He looked pale and ashy, sir—like something dead.

c.j. *faces* cobb.

c.j.: It's hard to breathe in these little spaces, Cobb—man wasn' made for this hea'—nothin' was! I don't think I'll eva' see a' animal in a cage agin' and not feel sorry for it. (*To himself*) I'd rather be on the chain gang.

cobb *looks up at him.*

cobb: Come on, homey! (*He rises, moves toward* c.j.)

c.j.: I don't think I'm comin' outta here, Cobb—feels like I'm goin' crazy. Can't walk in hea'—can't see the sun! I tried singin', Cobb, but nothin' won't come out. I sure don't wanna die in this jail!

cobb (*moving closer*): Ain't nobody gonna die, C.J.!

c.j.: Yesterday I broke a guitar string—lost my Dust! I got no protection—nothin' to keep the dog from tearin' at my bones!

cobb: Stop talkin' crazy!

c.j. *is quiet for a moment. He starts forward. Slowly, in center stage,* waters *emerges. He faces the audience.*

c.j.: You know, he come up hea' las' night? Sergeant Waters?

waters *smiles, pulls out his pipe, lights it.*

waters (*calmly*): You should learn never to hit sergeants, boy— man can get in a lot of trouble doin' that kinda thing durin' wartime—they talkin' 'bout givin' you five years—they call what you did mutiny in the navy. Mutiny, boy.

C.J.: That gun ain't mine!

WATERS: Oh, we know that, C.J.! (C.J. *is surprised*) That gun belonged to the niggah did the shootin' over at Williams's place—me and Wilkie caught him hidin' in the Motor Pool, and he confessed his head off. You're in here for striking a superior officer, boy. And I got a whole barracks full of your friends to prove it! (*Smiles broadly, as* C.J. *shakes his head*)

DAVENPORT (*to* COBB, *at once*): Memphis wasn't charged with the shooting?

COBB: No, sir—

WATERS: Don't feel too bad, boy. It's not your fault entirely—it has to be this way. The First War, it didn't change much for us, boy—but this one—it's gonna change a lot of things. Them Nazis ain't all crazy—a whole lot of people just can't fit into where things seem to be goin'—like you, C.J. The black race can't afford you no more. There use ta be a time when we'd see somebody like you, singin', clownin'—yas-sah-bossin'—and we wouldn't do anything. (*Smiles*) Folks liked that—you were good—homey kinda' niggah—they needed somebody to mis- treat—call a name, they paraded you, reminded them of the old days—corn-bread bakin', greens and ham cookin'—Daddy out pickin' cotton, Grandmammy sit on the front porch smokin' a pipe. (*Slight pause*) Not no more. The day of the geechy is gone, boy—the only thing that can move the race is power. It's all the white respects—and people like you just make us seem like fools. And we can't let nobody go on believin' we all like you! You bring us down—make people think the whole race is unfit! (*Quietly pleased*) I waited a long time for you, boy, but I gotcha! And I try to git rid of you wherever I go. I put two geechies in jail at Fort Campbell, Kentucky—three at Fort Huachuca. Now I got you—one less fool for the race to be ashamed of! (*Points*) And I'ma git that ole boy Cobb next! (*Light begins to fade around* WATERS)

DAVENPORT (*at once*): You?

COBB: Yes, sir. (*Slight pause*)

DAVENPORT: Go on.

C.J.: You imagin' anybody sayin' that? I know I'm not gittin' outta' hea', Cobb! (*Quiets*) You remember I tol' you 'bout a place I use ta go outside Carmella? When I was a little ole tiny thing? Place out behind O'Connell's Farm? Place would be stinkin' of plums, Cobb. Shaded—that ripe smell be weavin' through the cotton fields and clear on in ta town on a warm day. First time I had Evelyn? I had her unda' them plum trees. I wrote song a for her— (*Talks, sings*) My ginger-colored Moma —she had thighs the size of hams! (*Chuckles*) And when you spread them, Momaaaa! / (*Talks*) You let me have my jelly roll and jam! (*Pause, mood swing*) O'Connell, he had a dog— meanes' dog I *eva*' did see! An' the only way you could enjoy them plum trees was to outsmart that dog. Waters is like that ole dog, Cobb—you gotta run circles roun' ole Windy—that was his name. They say he tore a man's arm off once, and got to likin' it. So, you had to cheat that dog outta' bitin' you every time. Every time. (*Slowly the light begins to fade around* C.J.)

COBB: He didn't make sense, sir. I tried talkin' about the team— the war—ain't nothin' work—seem like he jes' got worse.

DAVENPORT: What happened to him?

COBB *looks at him incredulously.*

COBB: The next day—afta' the day I saw him? C.J., he hung his- self, sir! Suicide—jes' couldn't stand it. M.P.'s found him hung from the bars.

DAVENPORT *is silent for a moment.*

DAVENPORT: What happened after that?

COBB: We lost our last game—we jes' threw it—we did it for C.J.—Captain, he was mad 'cause we ain't git ta play the Yan- kees. Peterson was right on that one—somebody needed to pro- test that man!

DAVENPORT: What did Waters do?

COBB: Well, afta' we lost, the commanding officer, he broke up the team, and we all got reassigned to this Smoke Company. Waters, he started actin' funny, sir—stayed drunk—talked to hisself all the time.

DAVENPORT: Did you think you were next?

COBB: I ain't sure I eva' believed Waters said that, sir—C.J. had to be outta' his head or he wouldna' killed hisself—Sarge, he neva' came near me afta' C.J. died.

DAVENPORT: What time did you get back the night Waters was killed?

COBB: I'd say between 2120 and 9:30.

DAVENPORT: And you didn't go out again?

COBB: No, sir—me and Henson sat and listened to the radio till Abbott and Lou Costello went off, then I played checkers with Wilkie for 'notha' hour, then everybody went to bed. What C.J. said about Waters? It ain't botha' me, sir.

DAVENPORT *is silent.*

DAVENPORT: Who were the last ones in that night?

COBB: Smalls and Peterson—they had guard duty.

TAYLOR *enters the barracks area and stops just inside the door when he sees* DAVENPORT *isn't quite finished.*

DAVENPORT: Thank you, Corporal.

COBB *rises at attention and salutes.* DAVENPORT *returns salute and* COBB *starts out. He nods to* TAYLOR, *who advances toward* DAVENPORT.

TAYLOR *(smiling):* You surprise me, Davenport—I just left Colonel Nivens. He's given you permission to question Byrd and Wilcox? (DAVENPORT *nods*) How'd you manage that? You threatened him with an article in the Chicago *Defender,* I suppose.

DAVENPORT: I convinced the Colonel it was in his best interests to allow it.

TAYLOR: Really? Did he tell you I would assist you?

DAVENPORT: I told him I especially didn't want you.

TAYLOR: That's precisely why he sent me—he didn't want you to think you could get your way entirely—not with him. Then neither Byrd or Wilcox would submit to it without a white officer present. That's how it is. (*There is a rather long silence*) But there's something else, Davenport. The Colonel began talking about the affidavits he and the others signed—and the discrepancies in their statements that night. (*Mimics*) He wants me with you because he doesn't want Byrd and Wilcox giving you the wrong impression—he never elaborated on what he meant by the wrong impression. I want to be there!

DAVENPORT: So you're not on *that* side anymore—you're on *my* side now, right?

TAYLOR (*bristles*): I want whoever killed my sergeant, Davenport!

DAVENPORT: Bullshit! Yesterday you were daring me to try! And today we're allies? Besides, you don't give that much of a damn about your men! I've been around you a full day and you haven't uttered a word that would tell me you had any more than a minor acquaintance with Waters! He managed your baseball team—was an N.C.O. in your company, and you haven't offered *any* opinion of the man as a soldier—sergeant —platoon leader! Who the hell was he?

TAYLOR: He was one of my men! On my roster—a man these bars make me responsible for! And no, I don't know a helluva lot about him—or a lot of their names or where they come from, but I'm still their commanding officer and in a little while I may have to trust them with my life! And I want them to know they can trust me with theirs—here and now! (*Pause*) I have Byrd and Wilcox in my office. (DAVENPORT *stares at him for a long moment, then rises and starts out toward center stage*) Why didn't you tell Nivens that you'd placed me under arrest?

DAVENPORT *stops.*

DAVENPORT: I didn't find it necessary.

They stare at one another. TAYLOR *is noticeably strained.*

DAVENPORT (*starts away*): What do you know about C. J. Memphis?

TAYLOR *follows.*

TAYLOR (*shrugs*): He was a big man as I recall—more a boy than a man, though. Played the guitar sometimes at the Officers Club—there was something embarrassing about him. Committed suicide in the stockade. Pretty good center fielder—

DAVENPORT *stops.*

DAVENPORT: Did you investigate his arrest—the charges against him?

TAYLOR: He was charged with assaulting a noncommissioned officer—I questioned him—he didn't say much. He admitted he struck Waters—I started questioning several of the men in the platoon and he killed himself before I could finish—open-and-shut case.

DAVENPORT: I think Waters tricked C.J. into assaulting him.

TAYLOR: Waters wasn't that kind of a man! He admitted he might have provoked the boy—he accused him of that Golden Palace shooting—

Behind them, the CAPTAIN'*s office is lit. In two chairs facing* TAYLOR'*s desk are* LIEUTENANT BYRD *and* CAPTAIN WILCOX, *both in dress uniform.*

TAYLOR: Listen, Waters didn't have a fifth-grade education—he wasn't a schemer! And colored soldiers aren't devious like that.

DAVENPORT: What do you mean we aren't devious?

TAYLOR (*sharply*): You're not as devious—! (DAVENPORT *stares as* TAYLOR *waves disdainfully and starts into the office*) Anyway, what has that to do with this? (*He is distracted by* BYRD *and* WILCOX *before* DAVENPORT *can answer.* TAYLOR *speaks as he moves to his desk*) This is *Captain* Davenport—you've both been briefed by Colonel Nivens to give the Captain your full cooperation.

DAVENPORT *puts on his glasses.* TAYLOR *notices and almost smiles.*

BYRD (*to* DAVENPORT): They tell me you a lawyer, huh?

DAVENPORT: I am not here to answer your questions, Lieutenant. And I am Captain Davenport, is that clear?

BYRD (*to* TAYLOR): Captain, is he crazy?

TAYLOR: You got your orders.

BYRD: Sir, I vigorously protest as an officer—

TAYLOR (*cuts him off*): You answer him the way he wants you to, Byrd, or I'll have your ass in a sling so tight you won't be able to pee, soldier!

BYRD *backs off slightly.*

DAVENPORT: When did you last see Sergeant Waters?

BYRD: The night he was killed, but I didn' kill him—I should have blown his head off, the way he spoke to me and Captain Wilcox here.

DAVENPORT: How did he speak to you, Captain?

WILCOX: Well, he was very drunk—and he said a lot of things he shouldn't have. I told the Lieutenant here not to make the situation worse and he agreed, and we left the Sergeant on his knees, wallowing in self-pity. (*Shrugs*)

DAVENPORT: What exactly did he say?

WILCOX: Some pretty stupid things about us—I mean white people, sir.

BYRD *reacts to the term "sir."*

DAVENPORT: What kind of things?

BYRD (*annoyed*): He said he wasn't going to obey no white man's orders! And that me and Wilcox here were to blame for him being black, and not able to sleep or keep his food down! And I didn't even know the man! Never even spoke to him before that night!

DAVENPORT: Anything else?

WILCOX: Well—he said he'd killed somebody.

DAVENPORT: Did he call a name—or say who?

WILCOX: Not that I recall, sir.

DAVENPORT *looks at* BYRD.

BYRD: No— (*Sudden and sharp*) Look—the goddamn Negro was disrespectful! He wouldn't salute! Wouldn't come to attention! And where I come from, colored don't talk the way he spoke to us—not to white people they don't!

DAVENPORT: Is that the reason you killed him?

BYRD: I killed nobody! I said "where I come from," didn't I? You'd be dead yourself, where I come from! But I didn't kill the—the *Negro!*

DAVENPORT: But you hit him, didn't you?

BYRD: I knocked him down!

DAVENPORT (*quickens pace*): And when you went to look at him, he was dead, wasn't he?

BYRD: He was alive when we left!

DAVENPORT: You're a liar! You beat Waters up—you went back and you shot him!

BYRD: No! (*Rises*) But you better get outta my face before I kill you!

DAVENPORT *stands firm.*

DAVENPORT: Like you killed Waters?

BYRD: No! (*He almost raises a hand to* DAVENPORT)

TAYLOR (*at once*): Soldier!

BYRD: He's trying to put it on me!

TAYLOR: Answer his questions, Lieutenant.

DAVENPORT: You were both coming off bivouac, right?

WILCOX: Yes.

DAVENPORT: So you both had weapons?

BYRD: So what? We didn't fire them!

DAVENPORT: Were the weapons turned in immediately?

WILCOX: Yes, sir—Colonel Nivens took our .45's to Major Hines. It was all kept quiet because the Colonel didn't want the colored boys to know that anyone white from the Fort was involved in any way—ballistics cleared them.

DAVENPORT: We can check.

BYRD: Go ahead.

TAYLOR: I don't believe it—why wasn't I told?

WILCOX: The weapons had cleared—and the Colonel felt if he involved you further, you'd take the matter to Washington and there'd be a scandal about colored and white soldiers—as it turned out, he thinks you went to Washington anyway. (*To* DAVENPORT) I'd like to say, Captain, that neither Lieutenant Byrd or myself had anything whatsoever to do with Sergeant Waters's death—I swear that as an officer and a gentleman. He was on the ground when we left him, but very much alive.

TAYLOR: Consider yourselves under arrest, *gentlemen!*

BYRD: On what charge?

TAYLOR: Murder! You think I believe that crap—

DAVENPORT: Let them go, Captain.

TAYLOR: You've got motive—a witness to their being at the scene—

DAVENPORT: Let them go! This is still my investigation—you two are dismissed!

BYRD *rises quickly.* WILCOX *follows his lead.*

WILCOX: Are we being charged, sir?

DAVENPORT: Not by me.

WILCOX: Thank you.

WILCOX *comes to attention, joined by a reluctant* BYRD. *They both salute.* DAVENPORT *returns salute.*

BYRD: I expected more from a white man, Captain.

TAYLOR: Get out of here, before I have you cashiered out of the army, Byrd!

Both men exit quietly, and for a moment TAYLOR *and* DAVENPORT *are quiet.*

TAYLOR: What the hell is the matter with you? You could have charged both of them—Byrd for insubordination—Wilcox, tampering with evidence.

DAVENPORT: Neither charge is murder—you think Wilcox would tell a story like that if he didn't have Hines and Nivens to back it up? (*Slightly tired*) They've got a report.

TAYLOR: So what do you do now?

DAVENPORT: Finish the investigation.

TAYLOR: They're lying, dammit! So is the Colonel! You were ordered to investigate and charge the people responsible—charge them! I'll back you up!

DAVENPORT: I'm not satisfied yet, Captain.

TAYLOR: I am! Dammit!—I wish they'd sent somebody else! I do —you—you're afraid! You thought you'd accuse the Klan, didn't you?—and that would be the end of it, right? Another story of midnight riders for your Negro press! And now it's officers—white men in the army. It's too much for you—what will happen when Captain Davenport comes up for promotion to major if he accuses white officers, right?

DAVENPORT: I'm not afraid of white men, Captain.

TAYLOR: Then why the hell won't you arrest them?

DAVENPORT: Because I do what the facts tell me, Captain—not you!

TAYLOR: You don't know what a fact is, Davenport!

ELLIS *enters suddenly and salutes.*

ELLIS: Begging your pardon, sir.

TAYLOR: What is it, Corporal?

ELLIS: Ah—it's for Captain Davenport— (*To* DAVENPORT) We

found Private Wilkie, sir. We haven't located Pfc Peterson yet. Seems him and Private Smalls went out on detail together, and neither one of 'em showed up—but I got a few men from the company lookin' for 'em around the N.C.O. club and in the PX, sir.

DAVENPORT: Where's Wilkie?

ELLIS: He's waiting for you in the barracks, Captain.

DAVENPORT *nods, and* ELLIS *goes out after saluting. The lights come up around* WILKIE, *who is seated in a chair in the barracks reading a Negro newspaper.* DAVENPORT *is thoughtful for a moment.*

TAYLOR: Didn't you question Wilkie and Peterson yesterday? (DAVENPORT *starts out*) Davenport? (DAVENPORT *does not answer*) Don't you ignore me!

DAVENPORT: Get off my back! What I do—how I do it—who I interrogate is my business, Captain! This investigation is mine! (*Holds out the back of his hand, showing* TAYLOR *the color of his skin*) Mine!

TAYLOR: Don't treat me with that kind of contempt—I'm not some red-neck cracker!

DAVENPORT: And I'm not your yessirin' colored boy either!

TAYLOR: I asked you a question!

DAVENPORT: I don't have to answer it!

There is a long silence. The two men glare at one another— TAYLOR *in another time, disturbed.*

TAYLOR: Indeed you don't—*Captain.*

Pause.

DAVENPORT: Now, *Captain*—what if Byrd and Wilcox are telling the truth?

TAYLOR: Neither one of us believes that.

DAVENPORT: What if they are?

TAYLOR: Then who killed the goddamn man?

DAVENPORT: I don't know yet. (*Slight pause*) Is there anything else?

TAYLOR *shakes his head no as* DAVENPORT *starts toward center stage, headed toward* WILKIE.

TAYLOR: No, hotshot. Nothing.

DAVENPORT *enters the barracks area.* WILKIE *quickly puts his paper aside and snaps to attention and salutes.* DAVENPORT *returns salute but remains silent, going right to the desk and removing his pad and pencil. The light around the office fades out.*

DAVENPORT (*snapping at* WILKIE): When did you lose your stripes? (*He is standing over* WILKIE)

WILKIE: Couple months before they broke up the team—right after Sergeant Waters got assigned to us, sir.

DAVENPORT: Nervous, Wilkie?

WILKIE (*smiles haltingly*): I couldn't figure out why you called me back, sir? (*Laughs nervously*)

DAVENPORT: You lost your stripes for being drunk on duty, is that correct?

WILKIE: Yes, sir.

DAVENPORT: You said Waters busted you, didn't you?

WILKIE: He got me busted—he's the one reported me to the Captain.

DAVENPORT: How did you feel? Must have been awful— (DAVENPORT *paces*) Weren't you and the Sergeant good friends? Didn't you tell me he was all right? A nice guy?

WILKIE: Yes, sir.

DAVENPORT: Would a nice guy have gotten a friend busted?

WILKIE: No, sir.

DAVENPORT: So you lied when you said he was a nice guy, right?

WILKIE: No, sir—I mean—

DAVENPORT: Speak up! Speak up! Was the Sergeant a nice guy or not?

WILKIE: No, sir.

DAVENPORT: Why not? Answer me!

WILKIE: Well, you wouldn't turn somebody in over something like that!

DAVENPORT: Not a good friend, right?

WILKIE: Right, sir—I mean, a friend would give you extra duty— I would have—or even call you a whole buncha' names—you'd expect that, sir—but damn! Three stripes? They took ten years to get in this army, sir! Ten years! I started out with the 24th Infantry—I—

DAVENPORT: Made you mad, didn't it?

WILKIE: Yeah, it made me mad—all the things I did for him!

DAVENPORT (*quickly*): That's right! You were his assistant, weren't you? Took care of the team— (WILKIE *nods*) Ran all his errands, looked at his family snapshots (WILKIE *nods again*), policed his quarters, put the gun under C.J.'s bed—

WILKIE *looks up suddenly.*

WILKIE: No!

DAVENPORT (*quickly*): It was you Henson saw, wasn't it, Wilkie?

WILKIE: No, sir!

DAVENPORT: Liar! You lied about Waters, and you're lying now! You were the only person out of the barracks that night, and the only one who knew the layout well enough to go straight to C.J.'s bunk! Not even Waters knew the place that well! Henson didn't see who it was, but he saw what the person did—he was positive about that—only you knew the barracks in the dark!

WILKIE (*pleadingly*): It was the Sarge, Captain—he ordered me to do it—he said I'd get my stripes back—he wanted to scare that boy C.J.! Let him stew in jail! Then C.J. hit him—and he had the boy right where he wanted him— (*Confused*) But it backfired—C.J. killed hisself—Sarge didn't figure on that.

DAVENPORT: Why did he pick Memphis?

WILKIE: He despised him, Captain—he'd hide it, 'cause everybody in the company liked that boy so much. But underneath—it was a crazy hate, sir—he'd go cold when he talked about C.J. You could feel it.

In limbo, the blue-gray light rises on C.J. *and* WATERS. C.J. *is humming a blues song and* WATERS *is standing smiling, smoking a pipe as he was in Act One.* WATERS *turns away from* C.J. *His speech takes place over* C.J.'s *humming.*

WATERS: He's the kinda boy seems innocent, Wilkie. Got everybody around the post thinking he's a strong, black buck! Hits home runs—white boys envy his strength—his speed, the power in his swing. Then this colored champion lets those same white boys call him Shine—or Sambo at the Officers Club. They laugh at his blues songs, and he just smiles—can't talk, barely read or write his own name—and don't care! He'll tell you they like him—or that colored folks ain't supposed to have but so much sense. (*Intense*) Do you know the damage one ignorant *Negro* can do? (*Remembering*) We were in France during the First War, Wilkie. We had won decorations, but the white boys had told all the French gals we had tails. And they found this ignorant colored soldier. Paid him to tie a tail to his ass and parade around naked making monkey sounds. (*Shakes his head*) They sat him on a big, round table in the Café Napoleon, put a reed in his hand, a crown on his head, a blanket on his shoulders, and made him eat bananas in front of them Frenchies. And ohhh, the white boys danced that night— passed out leaflets with that boy's picture on them—called him Moonshine, King of the Monkeys. And when we slit his throat, you know that fool asked us what he had done wrong? (*Pause*) My daddy told me, we got to turn our backs on his kind, Wilkie. Close our ranks to the chittlin's, the collard greens— the corn-bread style. We are men—soldiers, and I don't intend to have our race cheated out of its place of honor and respect in *this* war because of fools like C.J.! You watch everything he does—*everything!*

Light fades slowly around WATERS *and* C.J., *and as it does,* C.J. *stops humming.*

WILKIE: And I watched him, sir—but Waters—he couldn't wait! He wouldn't talk about nothin' else—it was C.J. this—C.J. all the time!

DAVENPORT (*troubled*): Why didn't he pick Peterson—they fought—

WILKIE: They fought all the time, sir—but the Sarge, he likes Peterson. (*Nods*) Peterson fought back, and Waters admired that. He promoted Pete! Imagine that—he thought Peterson would make a fine soldier!

DAVENPORT: What was Peterson's reaction—when C.J. died?

WILKIE: Like everybody else, he was sad—he put together that protest that broke up the team, but afta' that he didn' say much. And he usually runs off at the mouth. Kept to himself—or with Smalls.

Slight pause.

DAVENPORT: The night Waters was killed, what time did you get in?

WILKIE: Around nine forty-five—couple of us came from the club and listened to the radio awhile—I played some checkers, then I went to bed. Sir? I didn't mean to do what I did—it wasn't my fault—he promised me my stripes!

Suddenly, out of nowhere, in the near distance, is the sound of gunfire, a bugle blaring, something like a cannon going off. The noise is continuous through scene. DAVENPORT *rises, startled.*

DAVENPORT: I'm placing you under arrest, Private!

ELLIS *bursts into the room.*

ELLIS: Did you hear, sir? (DAVENPORT, *surprised, shakes his head no*) Our orders! They came down from Washington, Captain! We're shippin' out! They finally gonna let us Negroes fight!

DAVENPORT *is immediately elated, and almost forgets* WILKIE *as he shakes* ELLIS's *hand.*

DAVENPORT: Axis ain't got a chance!

ELLIS: Surrrre—we'll win this mother in six months now! Afta' what Jesse Owens did to them people? Joe Louis?

HENSON *bursts in.*

HENSON: Did y'all hear it? Forty-eight-hour standby alert? We goin' into combat! (*Loud*) Look out, Hitler, the niggahs is comin' to git your ass through the fog!

ELLIS: With real rifles—it's really O.K., you know?

HENSON: They tell me them girls in England—woooow!

DAVENPORT *faces* WILKIE *as* COBB *enters, yelling.*

COBB: They gonna let us git in it! We may lay so much smoke the Germans may never get to see what a colored soldier looks like 'til the war's over! (*To* HENSON) I wrote my woman jes' the otha' day that we'd be goin' soon!

ELLIS: Go on!

HENSON (*overlapping*): Man, you ain't nothin'!

DAVENPORT *begins to move* WILKIE *toward* ELLIS.

HENSON: If the army said we was all discharged, you'd claim you wrote that! (*He quiets, watching* DAVENPORT)

COBB (*quickly*): You hea' this fool, sir?

HENSON: Shhhhh!

DAVENPORT (*To* ELLIS): Corporal, escort Private Wilkie to the
  stockade.

ELLIS (*surprised*): Yes, sir!

ELLIS *starts* WILKIE *out, even though he is bewildered by it. They
exit.*

HENSON: Wilkie's under arrest, sir? (DAVENPORT *nods*) How come?
  I apologize, sir—I didn't mean that.

DAVENPORT: Do either of you know where Smalls and Peterson
  can be located?

HENSON *shrugs.*

COBB: Your men got Smalls in the stockade, sir!

DAVENPORT: When?

COBB: I saw two colored M.P.'s takin' him through the main gate.
  Jes' a while ago—I was on my way ova' hea'!

DAVENPORT *goes to the desk and picks up his things and starts
out.*

COBB: Tenn-hut.

DAVENPORT *stops and salutes.*

DAVENPORT: As you were. By the way—congratulations!

DAVENPORT *exits the barracks through the doorway.*

HENSON: Look out, Hitler!

COBB: The niggahs is coming to get yo' ass.

HENSON AND COBB: Through the fog.

The lights in the barracks go down at once. Simultaneously, they rise in limbo, where SMALLS *is pacing back and forth. He is smoking a cigarette. There is a bunk, and the shadow of a screen over his cell. In the background, the sounds of celebration continue.* DAVENPORT *emerges from the right, and begins to speak immediately as the noises of celebration fade.*

DAVENPORT: Why'd you go AWOL, soldier?

SMALLS *faces him, unable to see* DAVENPORT *at first. When he sees him, he snaps to attention and salutes.*

SMALLS: Private Anthony Smalls, sir!

DAVENPORT: At ease—answer my question!

SMALLS: I didn't go AWOL, sir—I—I got drunk in Tynin and fell asleep in the bus depot—it was the only public place I could find to sleep it off.

DAVENPORT: Where'd you get drunk? Where in Tynin?

SMALLS: Jake's—Jake's and Lilly's Golden Slipper—on Melville Street—

DAVENPORT: Weren't you and Peterson supposed to be on detail? (SMALLS *nods*) Where was Peterson? Speak up!

SMALLS: I don't know, sir!

DAVENPORT: You're lying! You just walked off your detail and Peterson did nothing?

SMALLS: No, sir—he warned me, sir—"Listen, Smalls!" he said—

DAVENPORT (*cutting him off*): You trying to make a fool of me, Smalls? Huh? (*Loud*) Are you?

SMALLS: No, sir!

DAVENPORT: The two of you went A-W-O-L together, didn't you? (SMALLS *is quiet*) Answer me!

SMALLS: Yes!

DAVENPORT: You left together because Peterson knew I would find out the two of you killed Waters, didn' you? (SMALLS *suddenly bursts into quiet tears, shaking his head*) What? I can't hear you! (SMALLS *is sobbing*) You killed Waters, didn't you? I want an answer!

SMALLS: I can't sleep—I can't sleep!

DAVENPORT: Did you kill Sergeant Waters?

SMALLS: It was Peterson, sir! (*As if he can see it*) I watched! It wasn't me!

The blue-gray light builds in center stage. As it does, SERGEANT WATERS *staggers forward and falls on his knees. He can't get up, he is so drunk. He has been beaten, and looks the way we saw him in the opening of Act One.*

SMALLS: We were changing the guard.

WATERS: Can't be trusted—no matter what we do, there are no guarantees—and your mind won't let you forget it. (*Shakes his head repeatedly*) No, no, no!

SMALLS (*overlapping*): On our way back to the Captain's office —and Sarge, he was on the road. We just walked into him! He was ranting, and acting crazy, sir!

PETERSON *emerges from the right. He is dressed in a long coat, pistol belt and pistol, rifle, helmet, his pants bloused over his boots. He sees* WATERS *and smiles.* WATERS *continues to babble.*

PETERSON: Smalls, look who's drunk on his ass, boy! (*He begins to circle* WATERS)

SMALLS (*to* DAVENPORT): I told him to forget Waters!

PETERSON: Noooo! I'm gonna' enjoy this, Smalls—big, bad Sergeant Waters down on his knees? No, sah—I'm gonna' love this! (*Leans over* WATERS) Hey, Sarge—need some help? (WATERS *looks up; almost smiles. He reaches for* PETERSON, *who pushes him back down*) That's the kinda help I'll give yah, boy! Let me help you again—all right? (*Kicks* WATERS) Like that, Sarge? Huh? Like that, dog?

SMALLS (*shouts*): Peterson!

PETERSON: No! (*Almost pleading*) Smalls—some people, man— If this was a German, would you kill it? If it was Hitler—or that fuckin' Tojo? Would you kill him? (*Kicks* WATERS *again*)

WATERS (*mumbling throughout*): There's a trick to it, Peterson— it's the only way you can win—C.J. could never make it—he was a clown! (*Grabs at* PETERSON) A clown in blackface! A niggah!

PETERSON *steps out of reach. He is suddenly expressionless as he easily removes his pistol from his holster.*

WATERS: You got to be like them! And I was! I was—but the rules are fixed. (*Whispers*) Shhhh! Listen. It's C.J.— (*Laughs*) I made him do it, but it doesn't make any difference! They still hate you! (*Looks at* PETERSON, *who has moved closer to him*) They still hate you! (WATERS *laughs*)

PETERSON (*to* SMALLS): Justice, Smalls. (*He raises the pistol*)

DAVENPORT (*suddenly, harshly*): That isn't justice!

SMALLS *almost recoils.*

PETERSON (*simultaneously, continuing*): For C.J.! Everybody!

PETERSON *fires the gun at* WATERS's *chest, and the shot stops every-thing. The celebration noise stops. Even* DAVENPORT *in his way seems to hear it.* PETERSON *fires again. There is a moment of quiet on stage.* DAVENPORT *is angered and troubled.*

DAVENPORT: You call that justice?

SMALLS: No, sir.

DAVENPORT (*enraged*): Then why the fuck didn't you do some-thing?

SMALLS: I'm scared of Peterson—just scared of him!

PETERSON *has been looking at* WATERS's *body throughout. He now begins to lift* WATERS *as best he can, and pull him off-stage. It is done with some difficulty.*

SMALLS: I tried to get him to go, sir, but he wanted to drag the Sergeant's body back into the woods—

Light fades quickly around PETERSON, *as* DAVENPORT *paces.*

SMALLS: Said everybody would think white people did it.

DAVENPORT (*somewhat drained*): Then what happened?

SMALLS: I got sick, sir—and Peterson, when he got done, he helped me back to the barracks and told me to keep quiet. (*Slight pause*) I'm sorry, sir.

There is a long pause, during which DAVENPORT *stares at* SMALLS *with disgust, then abruptly starts out without saluting. He almost flees.* SMALLS *rises quickly.*

SMALLS: Sir?

DAVENPORT *turns around.* SMALLS *comes to attention and salutes.* DAVENPORT *returns salute and starts out of the cell and down toward center stage. He is thoughtful as the light fades around* SMALLS. DAVENPORT *removes his glasses and begins to clean them as he speaks.*

DAVENPORT: Peterson was apprehended a week later in Alabama. Colonel Nivens called it "just another black mess of cuttin', slashin', and shootin'!" He was delighted there were no white officers mixed up in it, and his report to Washington characterized the events surrounding Waters's murder as "the usual, common violence any commander faces in Negro Military units." It was the kind of "mess" that turns up on page 3 in the colored papers—the Cain and Abel story of the week—the headline we Negroes can't quite read in comfort. (*Shakes head and paces*) For me? Two colored soldiers are dead—two on their way to prison. Four less men to fight with—and none of their reasons—nothing anyone *said,* or *did,* would have been worth a life to men with larger hearts—men less split by the madness of race in America. (*Pause*) The case got little attention. The details were filed in my report and I was quickly and rather unceremoniously ordered back to my M.P. unit. (*Smiles*) A style of guitar pickin' and a dance called the C.J. caught on for a while in Tynin saloons during 1945. (*Slight pause*) In northern New Jersey, through a military foul-up, Sergeant Waters's family was informed that he had been killed in action. The Sergeant was, therefore, thought and unofficially rumored to have been the first colored casualty of the war from that county and under the circumstances was declared a hero. Nothing could be done officially, but his picture was hung on a Wall of Honor in the Dorie Miller VFW Post #978. (*Pause*) The men of the 221st Chemical Smoke Generating Company? The entire outfit—officers and enlisted men—was wiped out in the Ruhr Valley during a German advance. (*He turns toward* TAYLOR, *who enters quietly*) Captain?

TAYLOR: Davenport—I see you got your man.

DAVENPORT: I got him—what is it, Captain?

TAYLOR: Will you accept my saying, you did a splendid job?

DAVENPORT: I'll take the praise—but how did I manage it?

TAYLOR: Dammit, Davenport—I didn't come here to be made fun of— (*Slight pause*) The men—the regiment—we all ship out for Europe tomorrow, and (*hesitates*) I was wrong, Davenport—about the bars—the uniform—about Negroes being in charge. (*Slight pause*) I guess I'll *have* to get used to it.

DAVENPORT: Oh, you'll get used to it—you can bet your ass on that. Captain—you will get used to it.

Lights begin to fade slowly as the music "Don't Sit under the Apple Tree" rises in the background, and the house goes to black.